The Benz and Foiles Families of Illinois.

Germany & England

Linda Roe Karle

Dedication

Dear Family,

Over the past three years of working independently, and then hiring help from a professional Genealogist, I have completed our family history to the best of my ability.

The research in this book was done by using public documents, such as census, marriage, birth and death records with various Ancestry Databases. I made many research contacts at Texas Archives in which I received historic information and documented papers that I scanned into various records.

I am thankful to all my past and present family members who were so kind to me whenever I asked for help confirming my questions.

I hope you find this book interesting.

Yours Truly

May 2017

Abbreviations

ABBREVIATIONS

DAR Daughters of the American Revolution

SAR Sons of the American Revolution

FFA First Families of America

SCV Sons of Confederate Veterans

UDC United Daughters of the Confederacy

SDT Sons and Daughters of Texas

NOTE: The older family members are direct lines back brother and sisters are omitted for space reasons only.

Table of Contents

Table of Contents

Family Tree Chart for Wanda Lucille Benz

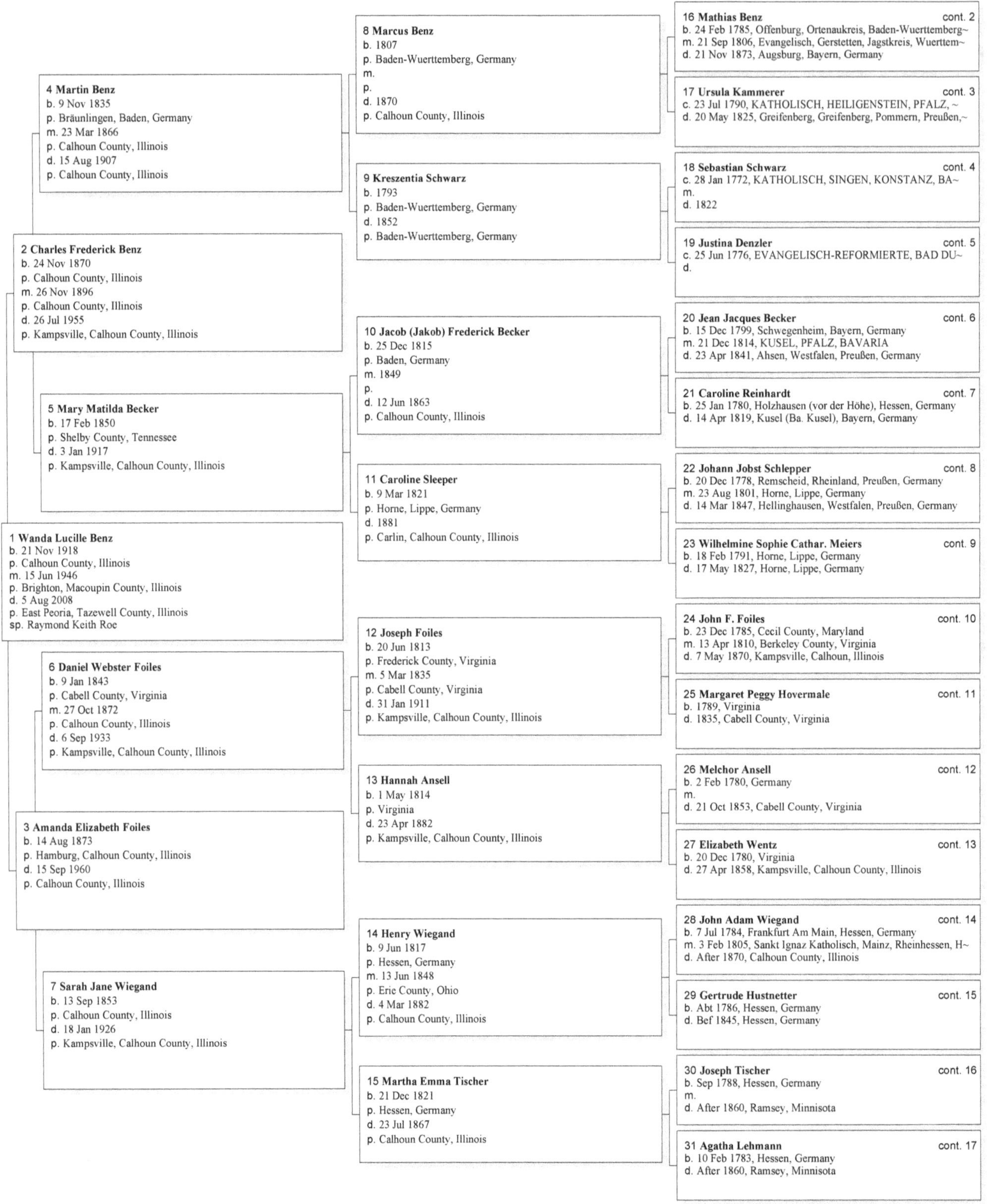

Family Tree Chart for Mathias Benz

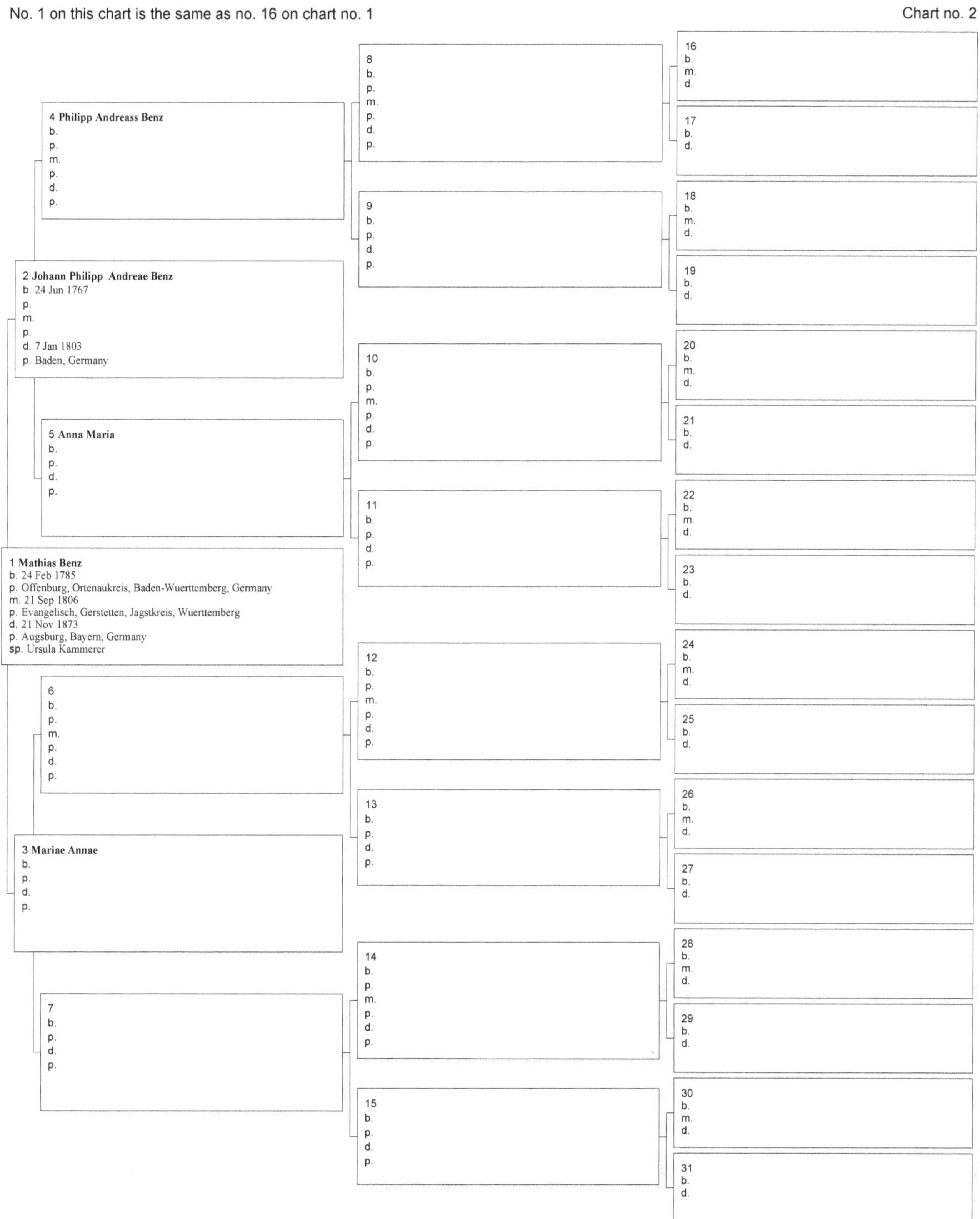

Family Tree Chart for Ursula Kammerer

No. 1 on this chart is the same as no. 17 on chart no. 1

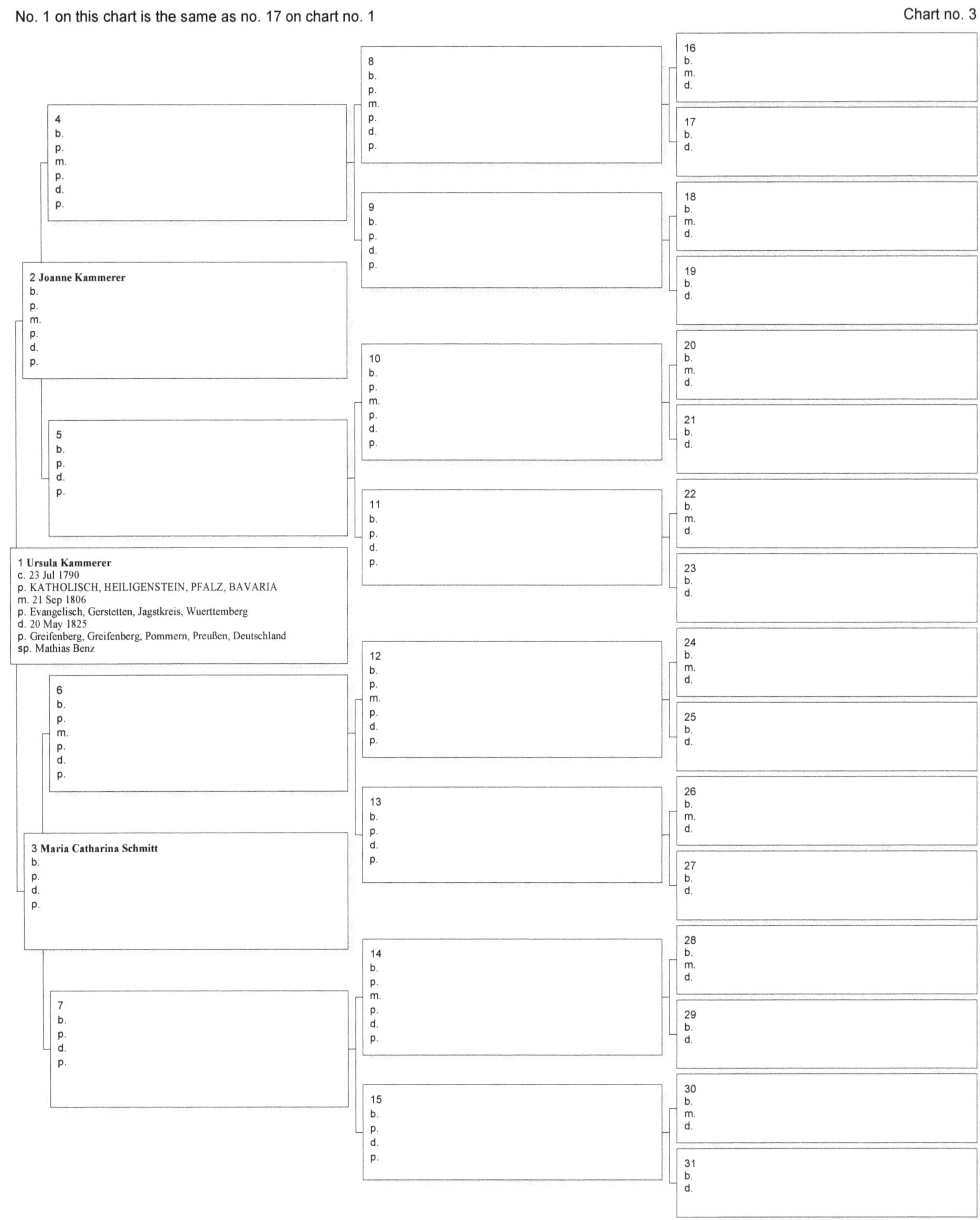

Family Tree Chart for Sebastian Schwarz

No. 1 on this chart is the same as no. 18 on chart no. 1

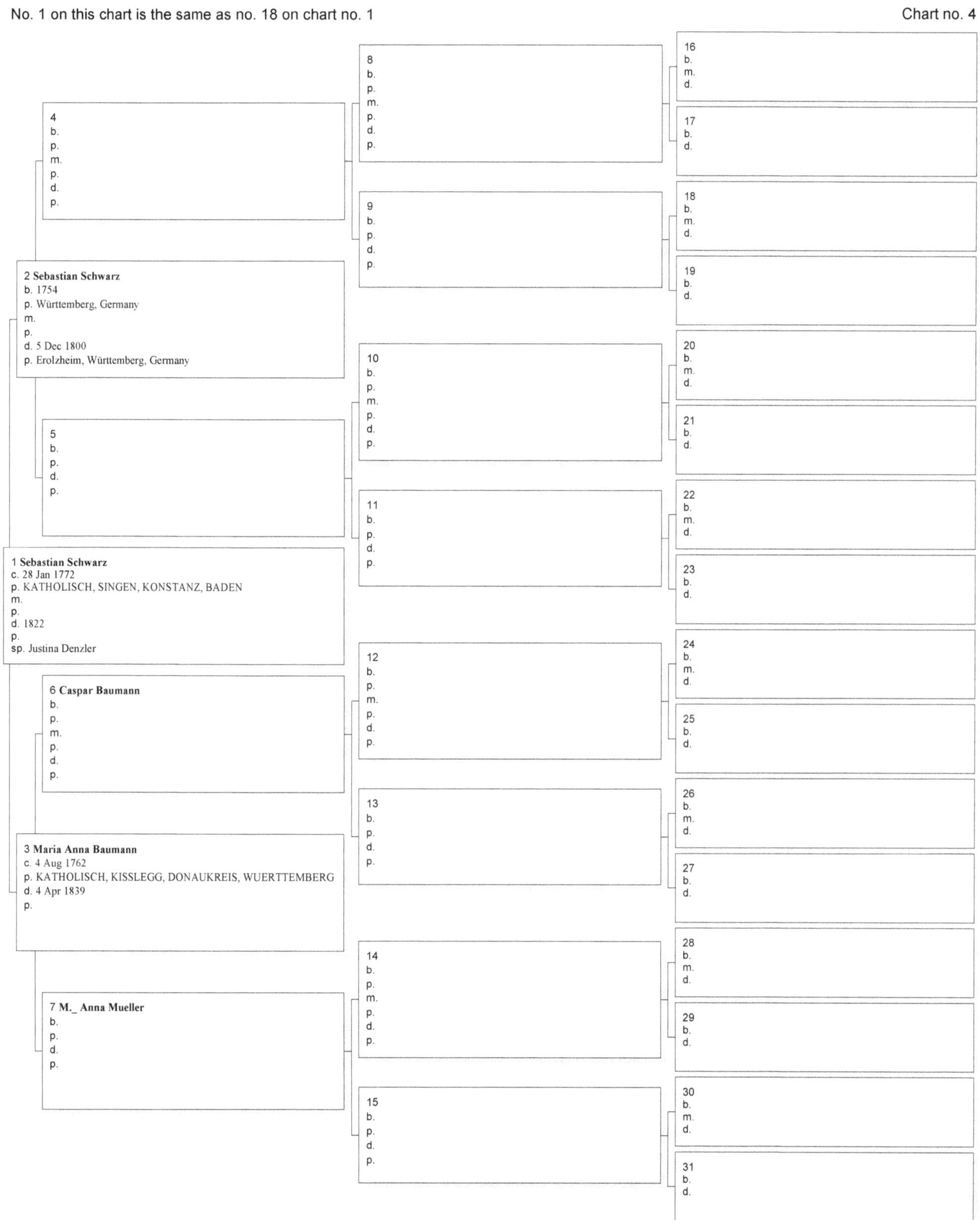

Family Tree Chart for Justina Denzler

No. 1 on this chart is the same as no. 19 on chart no. 1

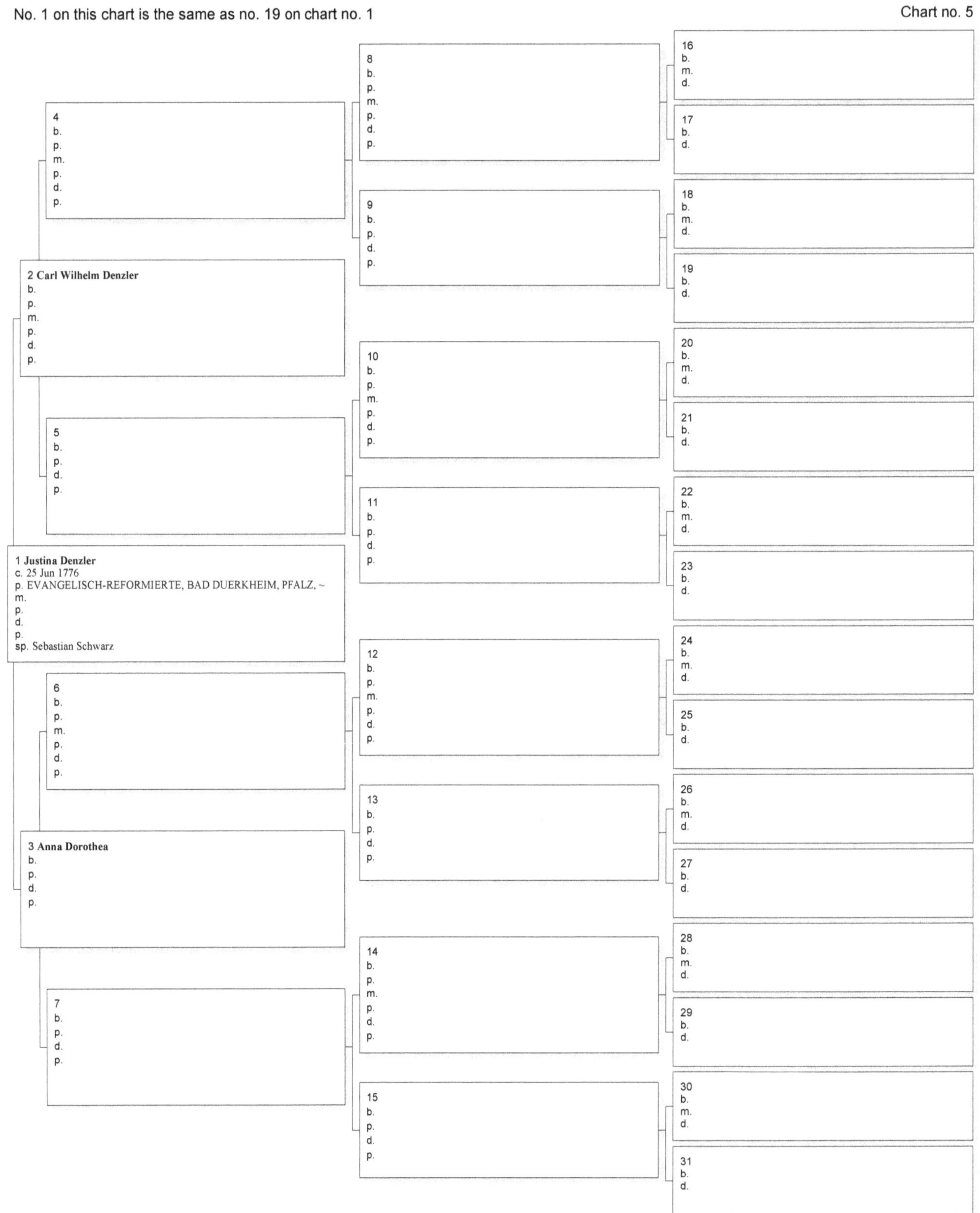

No. 1 on this chart is the same as no. 20 on chart no. 1

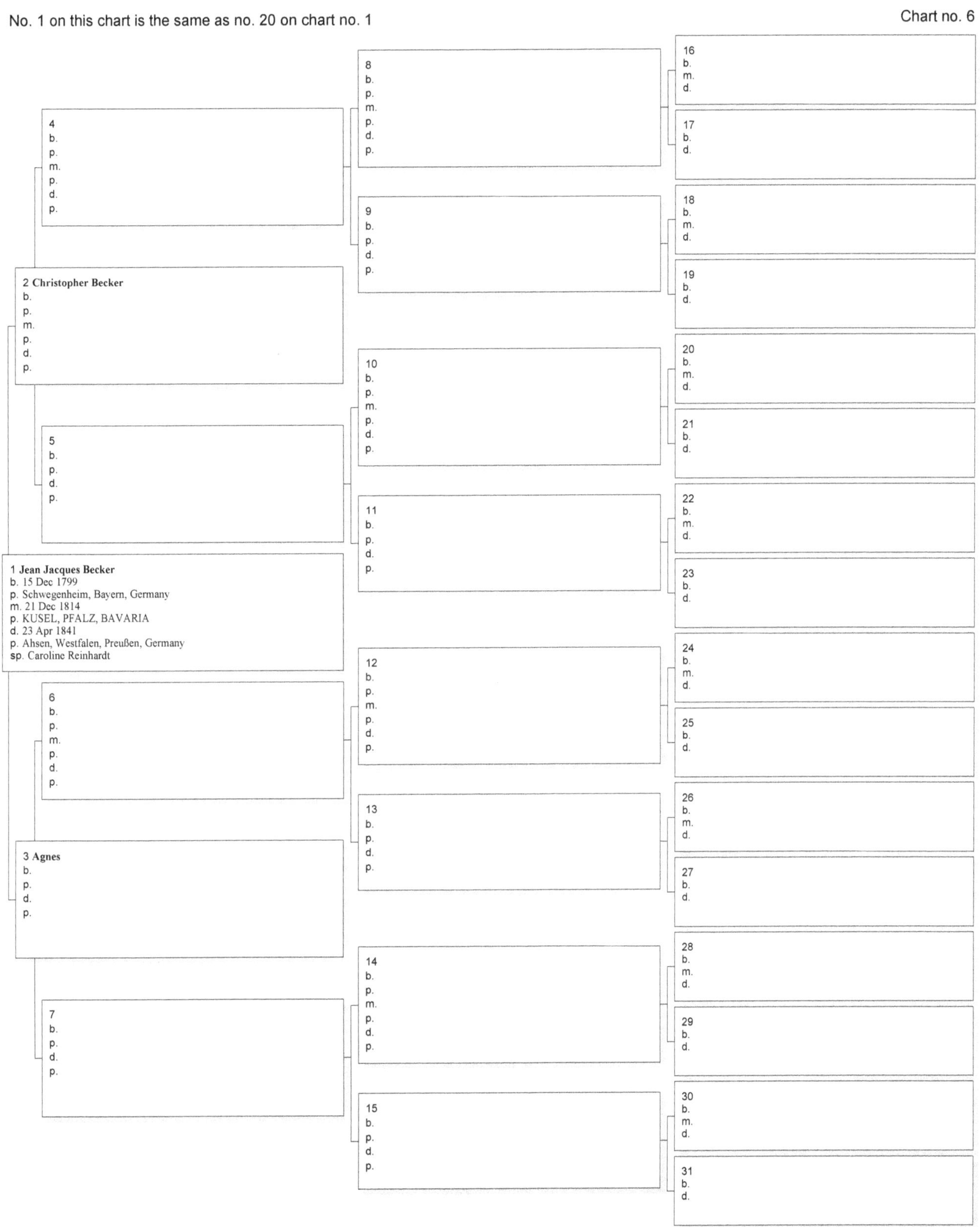

Family Tree Chart for Caroline Reinhardt

No. 1 on this chart is the same as no. 21 on chart no. 1

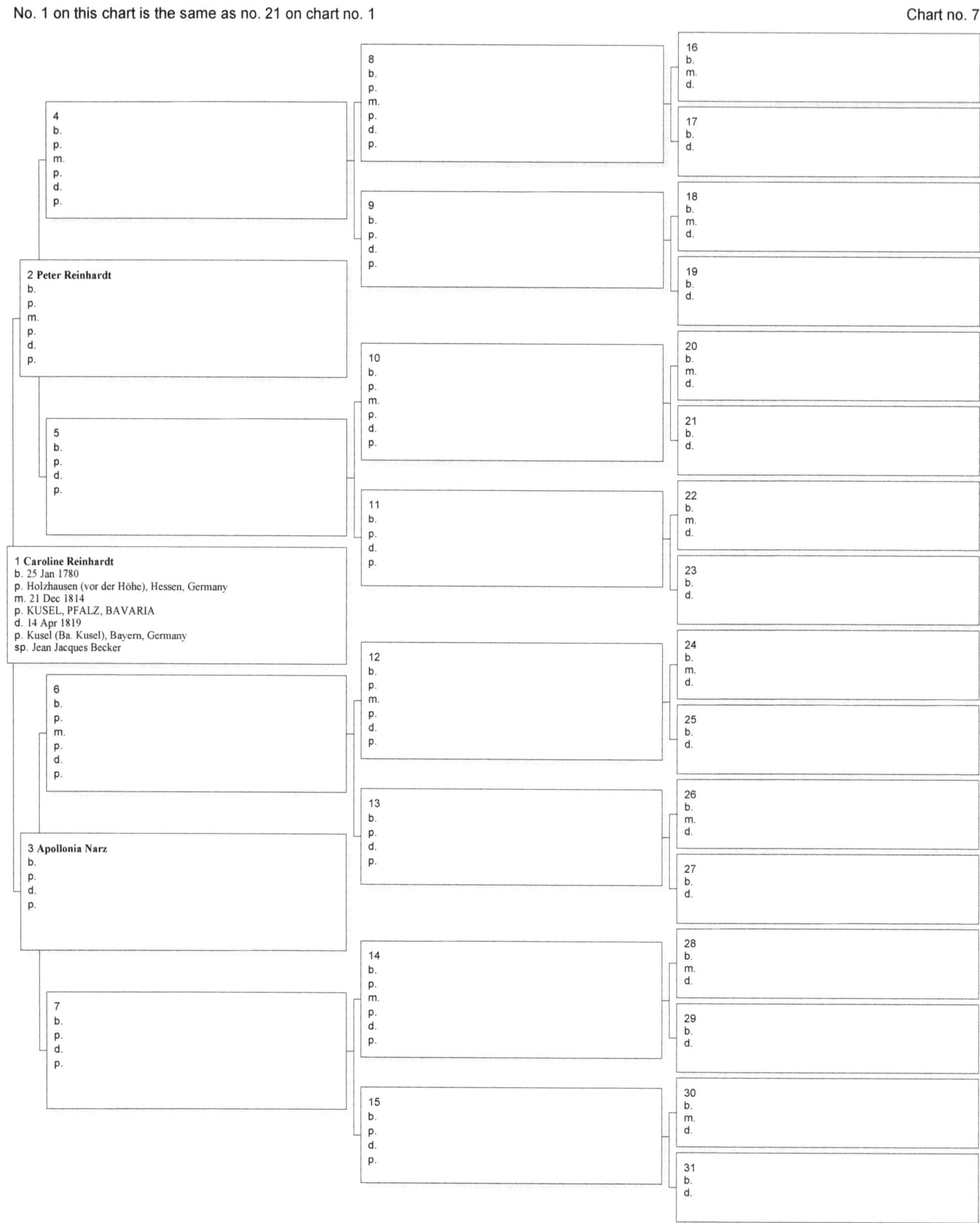

Family Tree Chart for Johann Jobst Schlepper

No. 1 on this chart is the same as no. 22 on chart no. 1

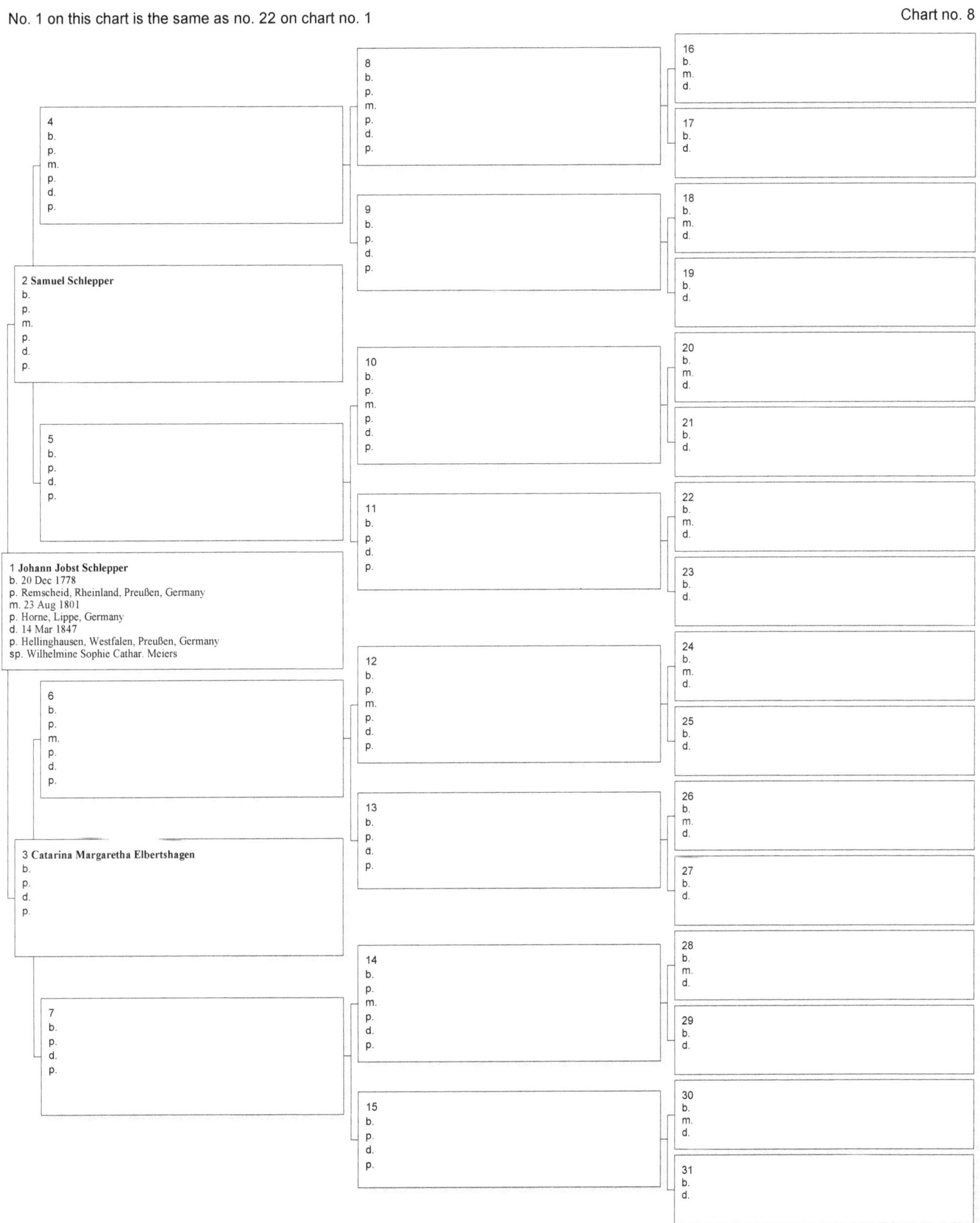

Family Tree Chart for Wilhelmine Sophie Cathar. Meiers

No. 1 on this chart is the same as no. 23 on chart no. 1

Chart no. 9

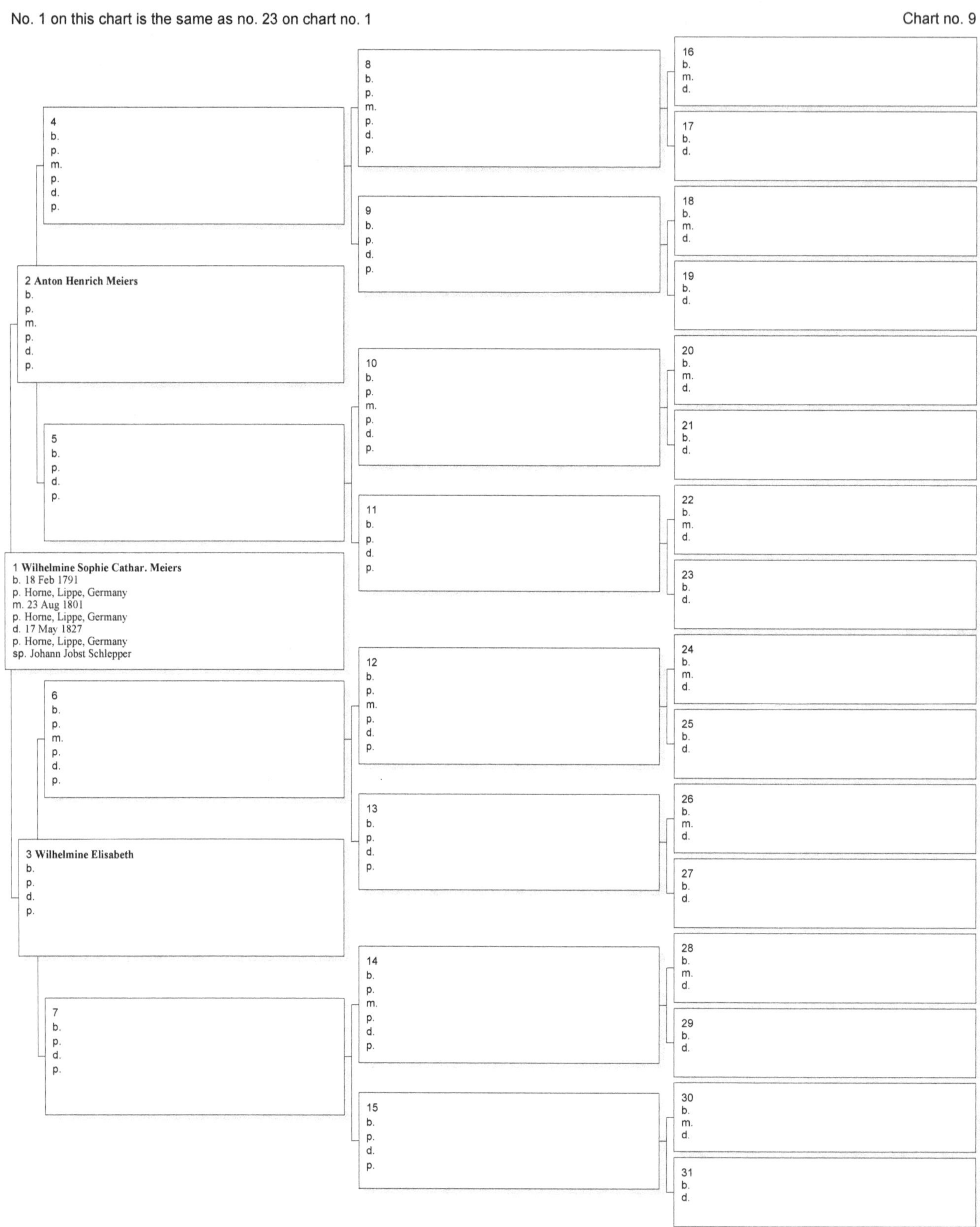

Family Tree Chart for John F. Foiles

No. 1 on this chart is the same as no. 24 on chart no. 1

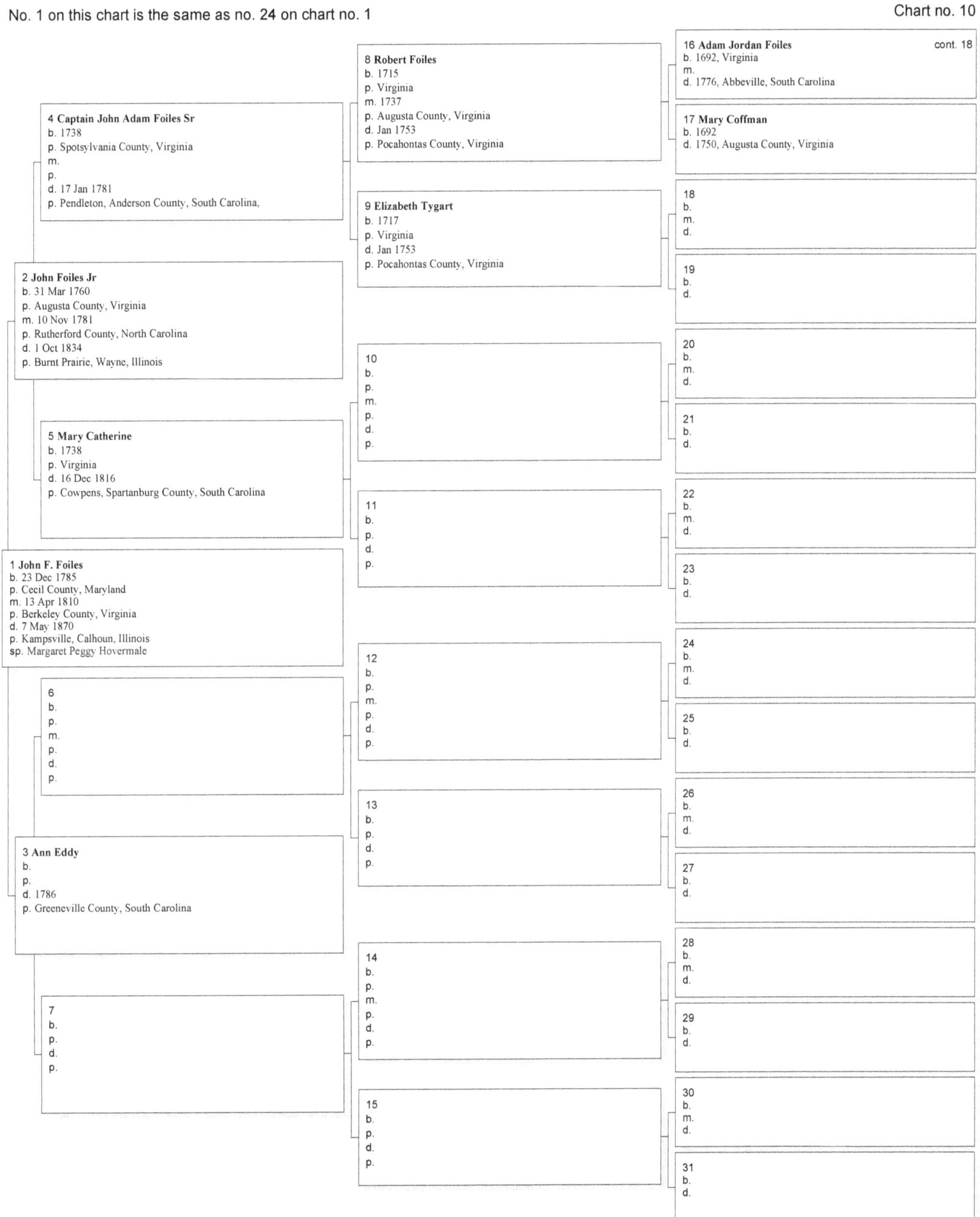

4 Captain John Adam Foiles Sr
b. 1738
p. Spotsylvania County, Virginia
m.
p.
d. 17 Jan 1781
p. Pendleton, Anderson County, South Carolina,

2 John Foiles Jr
b. 31 Mar 1760
p. Augusta County, Virginia
m. 10 Nov 1781
p. Rutherford County, North Carolina
d. 1 Oct 1834
p. Burnt Prairie, Wayne, Illinois

5 Mary Catherine
b. 1738
p. Virginia
d. 16 Dec 1816
p. Cowpens, Spartanburg County, South Carolina

1 John F. Foiles
b. 23 Dec 1785
p. Cecil County, Maryland
m. 13 Apr 1810
p. Berkeley County, Virginia
d. 7 May 1870
p. Kampsville, Calhoun, Illinois
sp. Margaret Peggy Hovermale

6
b.
p.
m.
p.
d.
p.

3 Ann Eddy
b.
p.
d. 1786
p. Greeneville County, South Carolina

7
b.
p.
d.
p.

8 Robert Foiles
b. 1715
p. Virginia
m. 1737
p. Augusta County, Virginia
d. Jan 1753
p. Pocahontas County, Virginia

9 Elizabeth Tygart
b. 1717
p. Virginia
d. Jan 1753
p. Pocahontas County, Virginia

10
b.
p.
m.
p.
d.
p.

11
b.
p.
d.
p.

12
b.
p.
m.
p.
d.
p.

13
b.
p.
d.
p.

14
b.
p.
m.
p.
d.
p.

15
b.
p.
d.
p.

16 Adam Jordan Foiles cont. 18
b. 1692, Virginia
m.
d. 1776, Abbeville, South Carolina

17 Mary Coffman
b. 1692
d. 1750, Augusta County, Virginia

18
b.
m.
d.

19
b.
d.

20
b.
m.
d.

21
b.
d.

22
b.
m.
d.

23
b.
d.

24
b.
m.
d.

25
b.
d.

26
b.
m.
d.

27
b.
d.

28
b.
m.
d.

29
b.
d.

30
b.
m.
d.

31
b.
d.

No. 1 on this chart is the same as no. 25 on chart no. 1

Chart no. 11

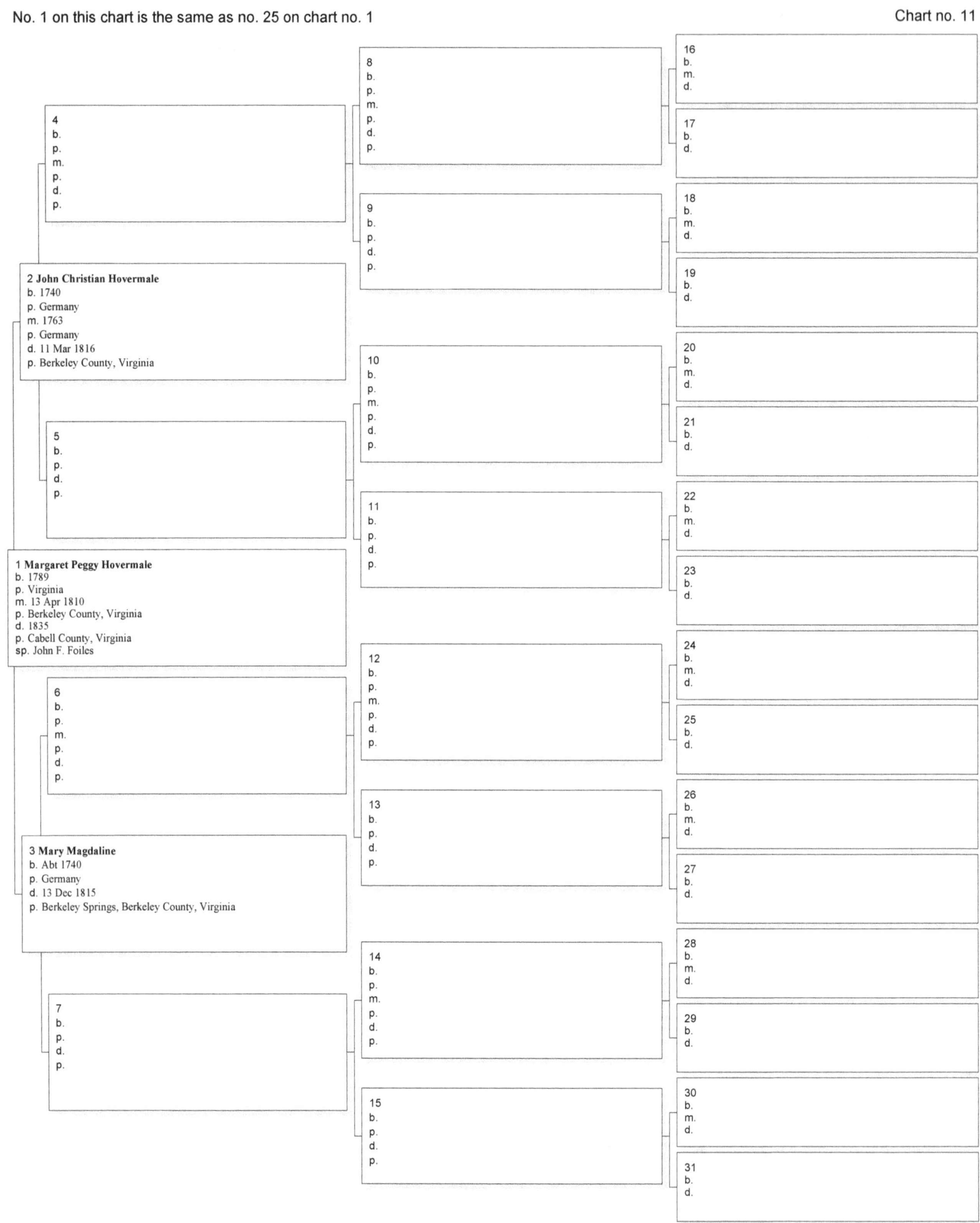

Family Tree Chart for Melchor Ansell

No. 1 on this chart is the same as no. 26 on chart no. 1

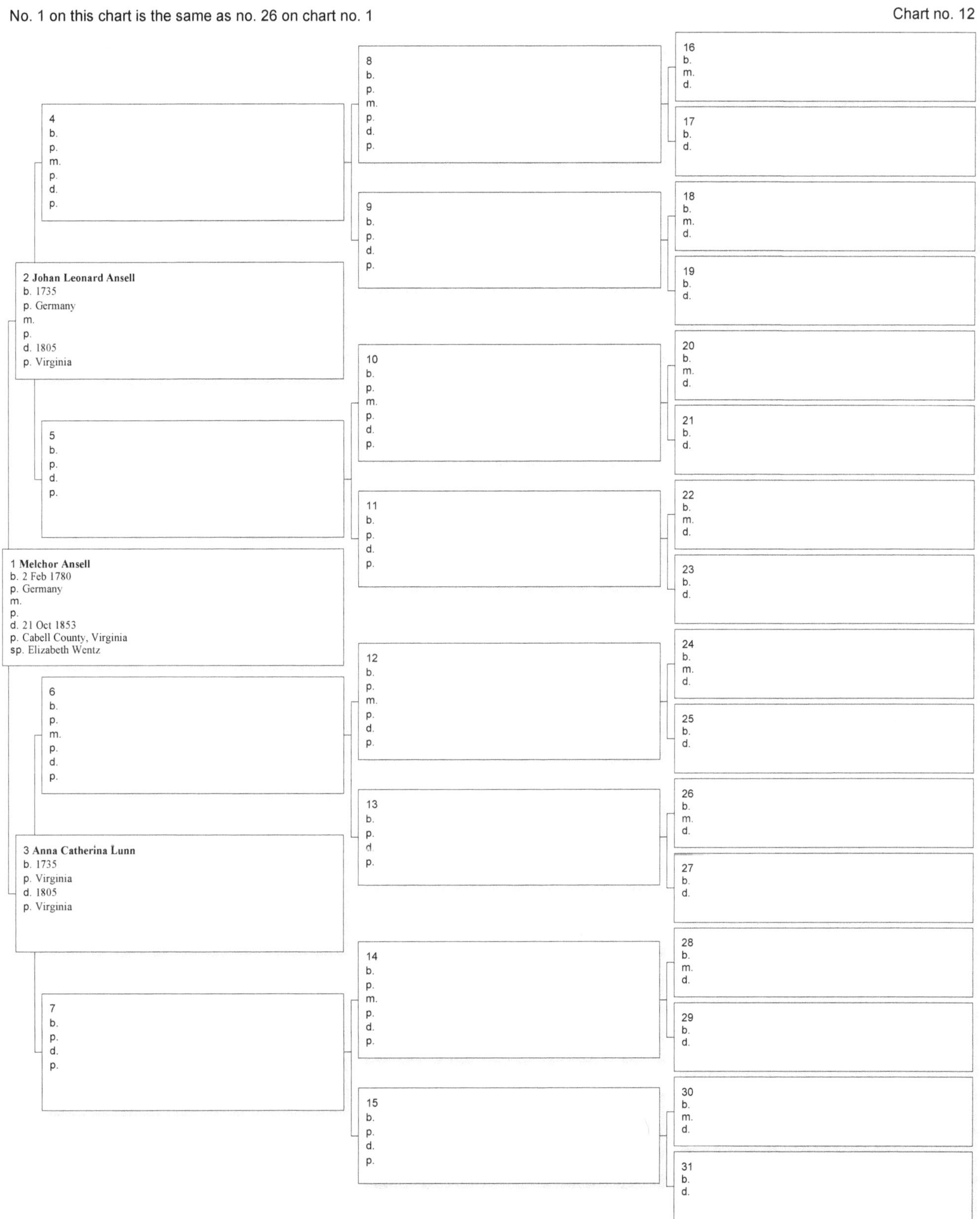

Family Tree Chart for Elizabeth Wentz

No. 1 on this chart is the same as no. 27 on chart no. 1

Chart no. 13

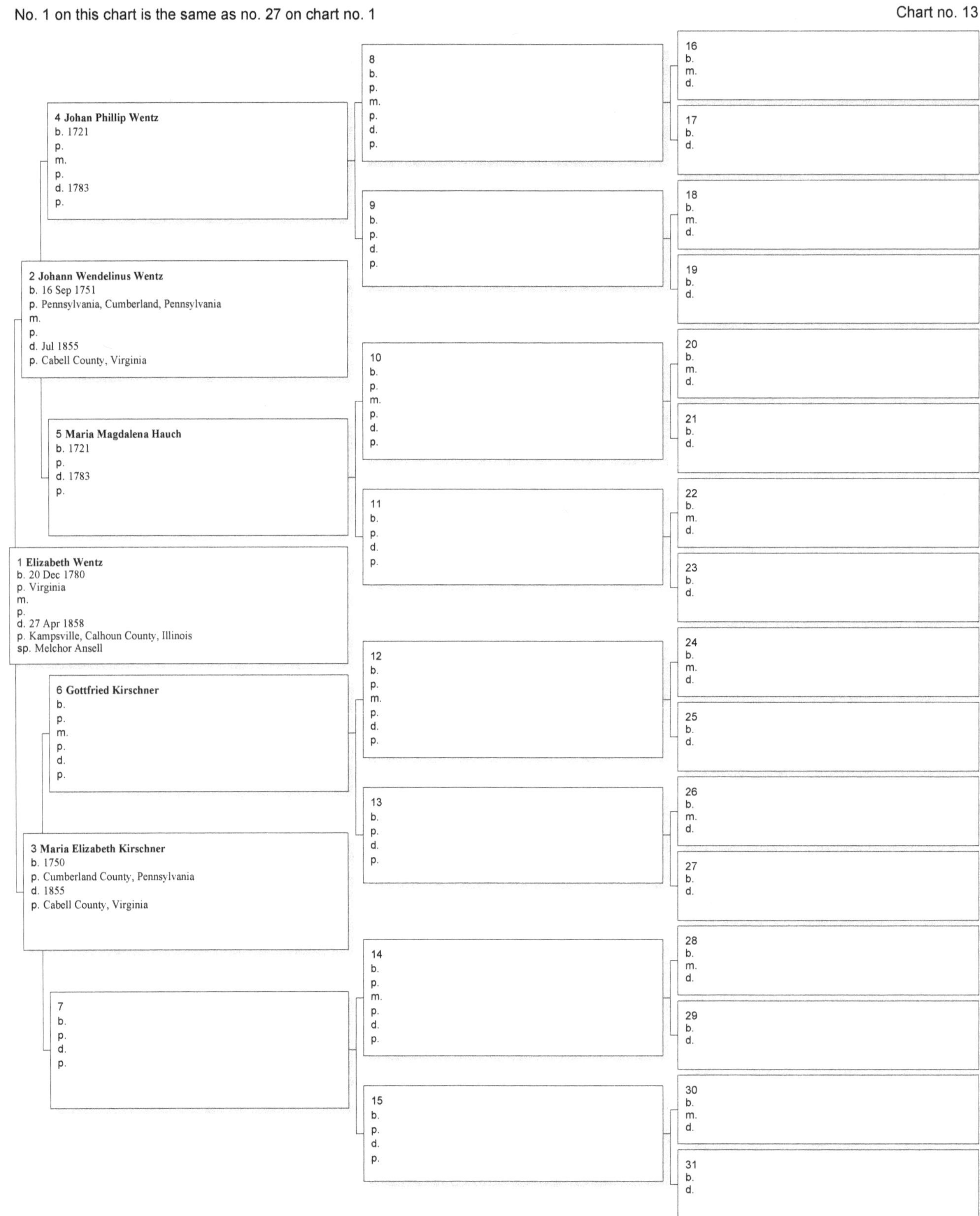

Family Tree Chart for John Adam Wiegand

No. 1 on this chart is the same as no. 28 on chart no. 1

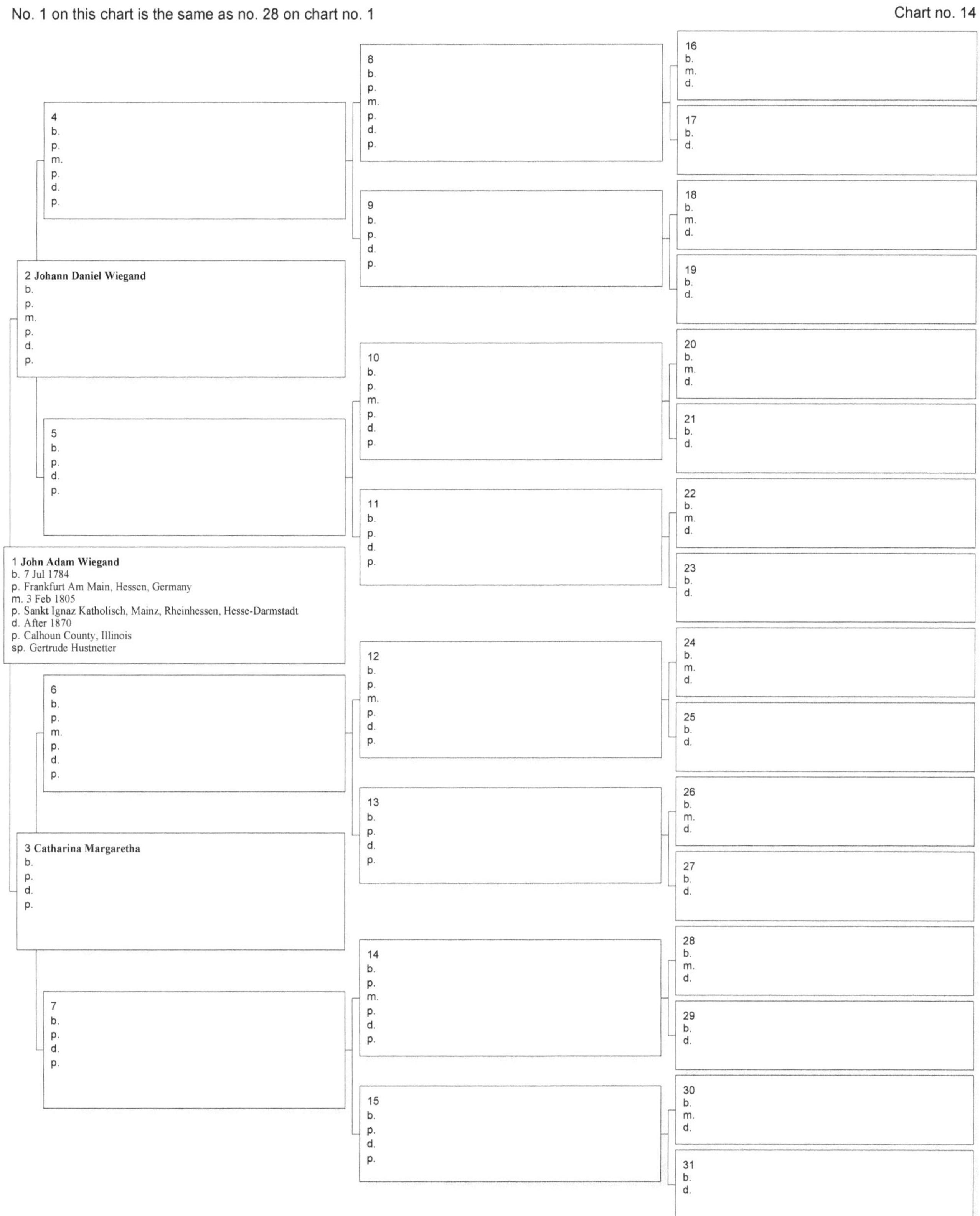

No. 1 on this chart is the same as no. 29 on chart no. 1

Chart no. 15

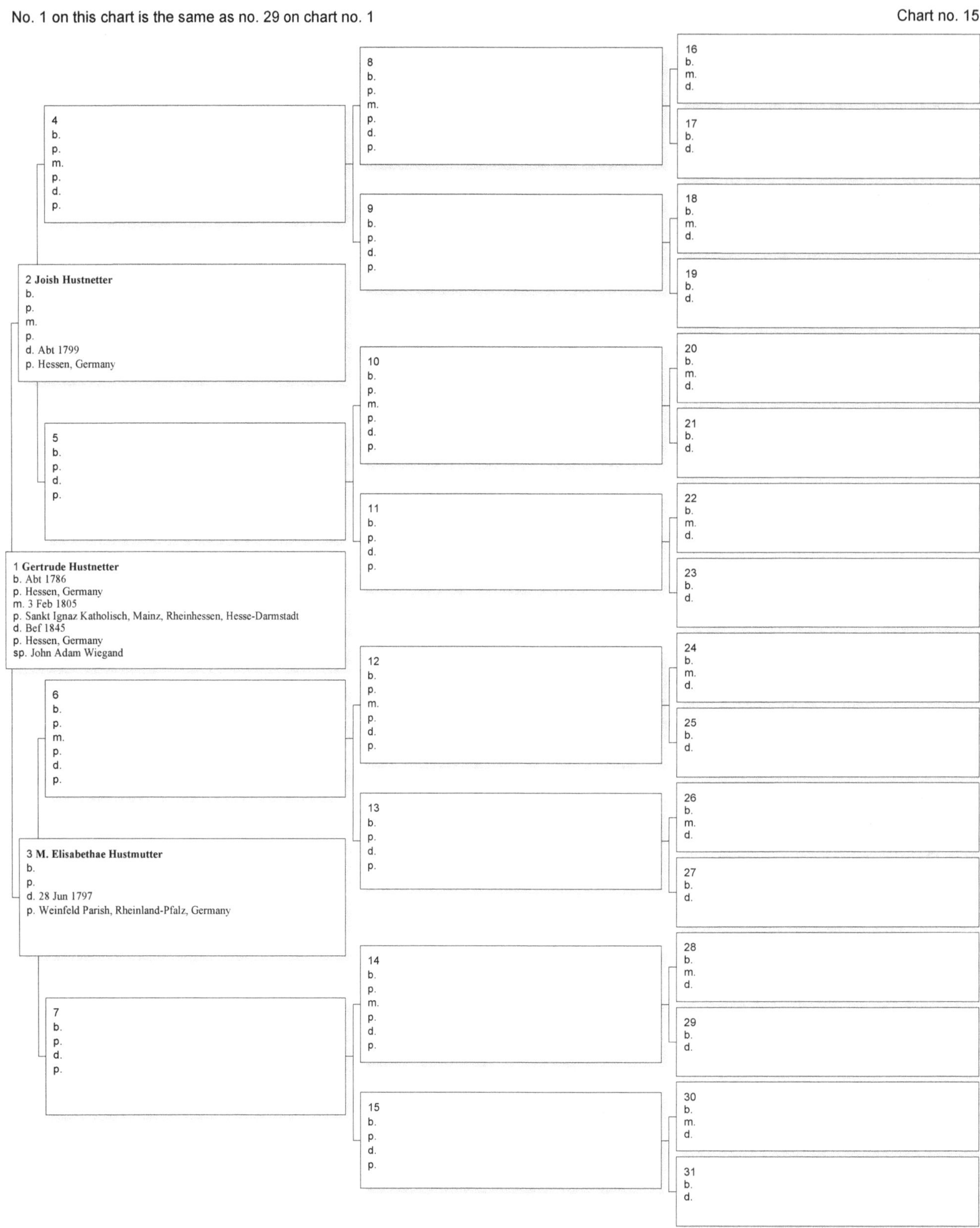

No. 1 on this chart is the same as no. 30 on chart no. 1

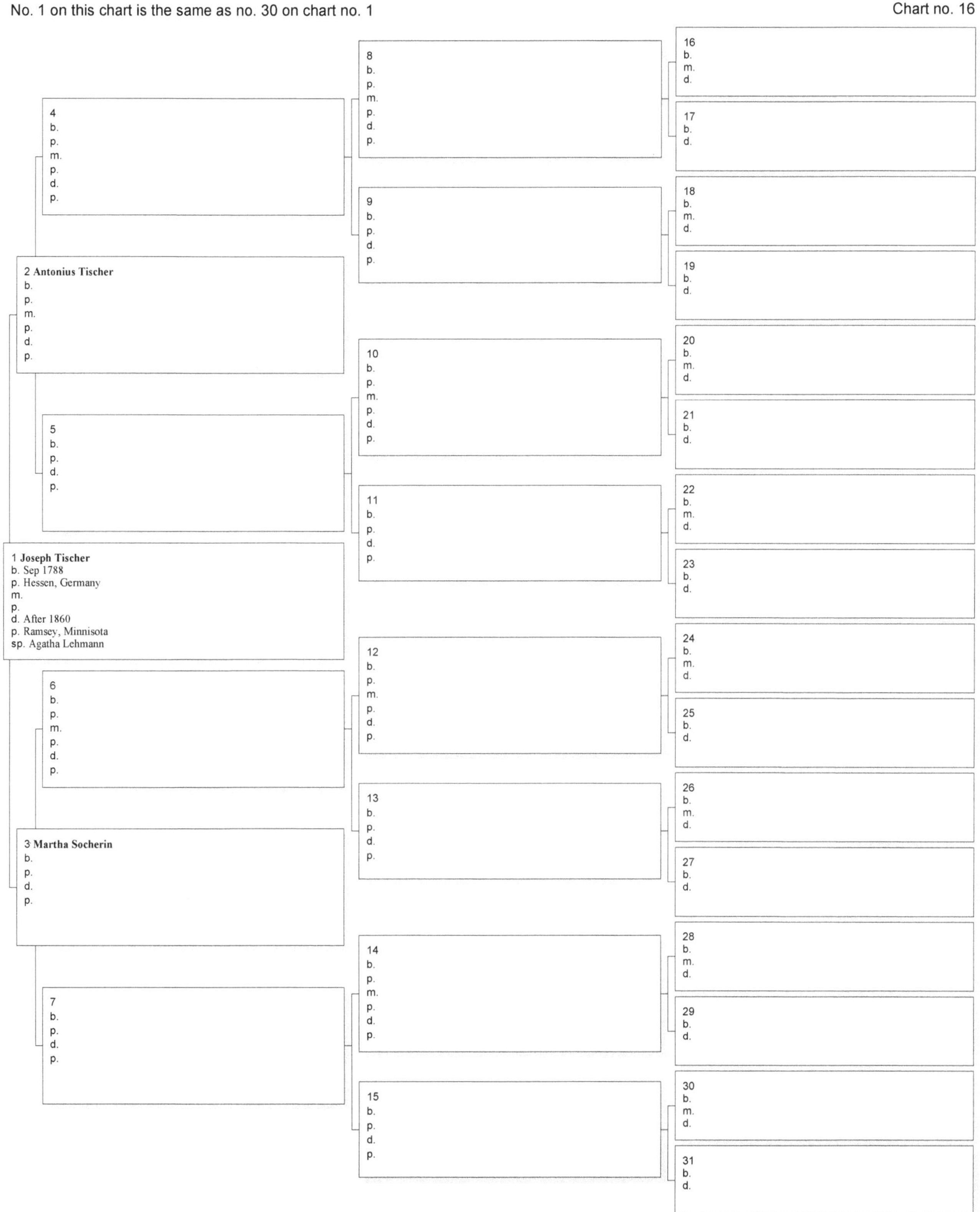

No. 1 on this chart is the same as no. 31 on chart no. 1

Chart no. 17

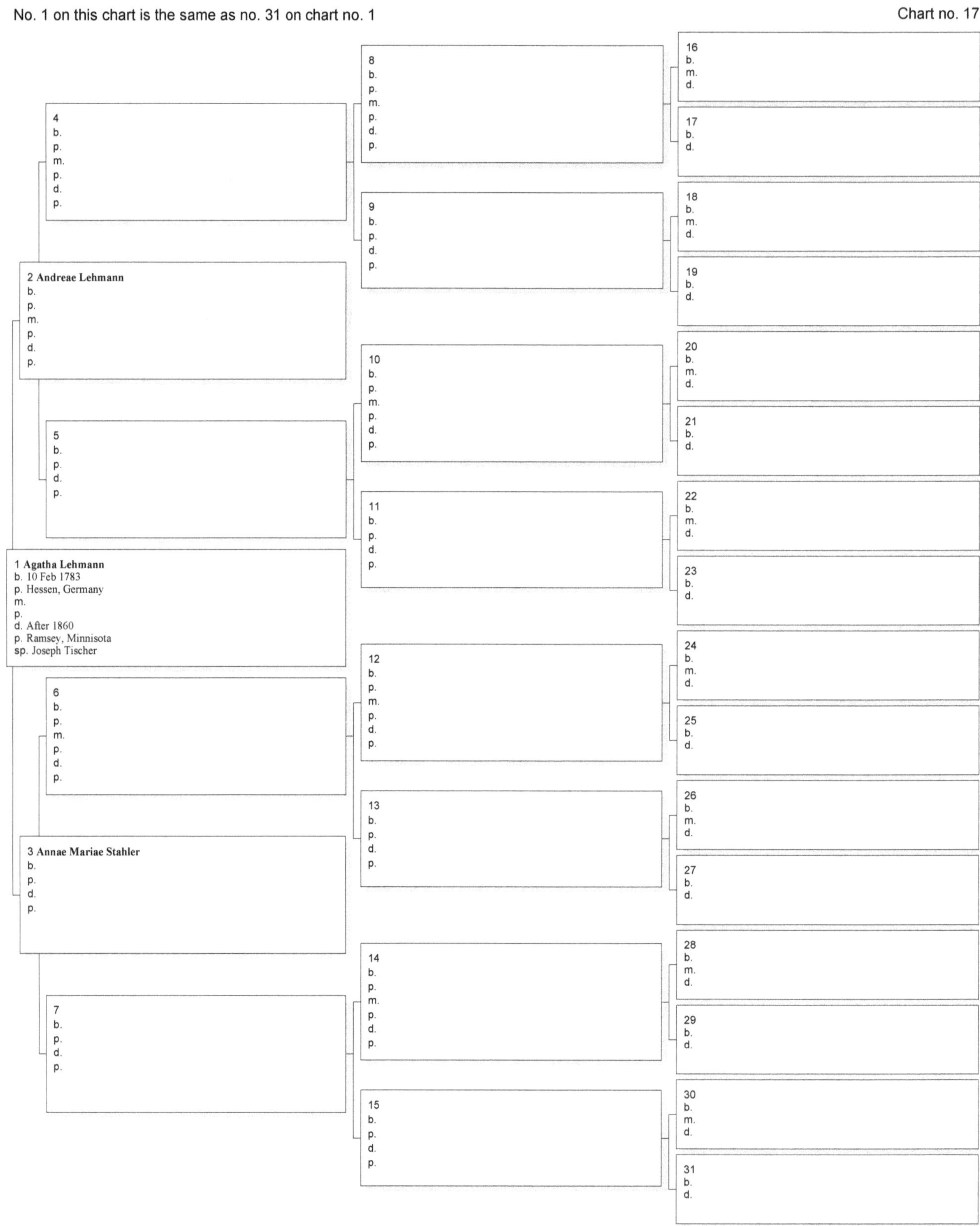

No. 1 on this chart is the same as no. 16 on chart no. 10

Chart no. 18

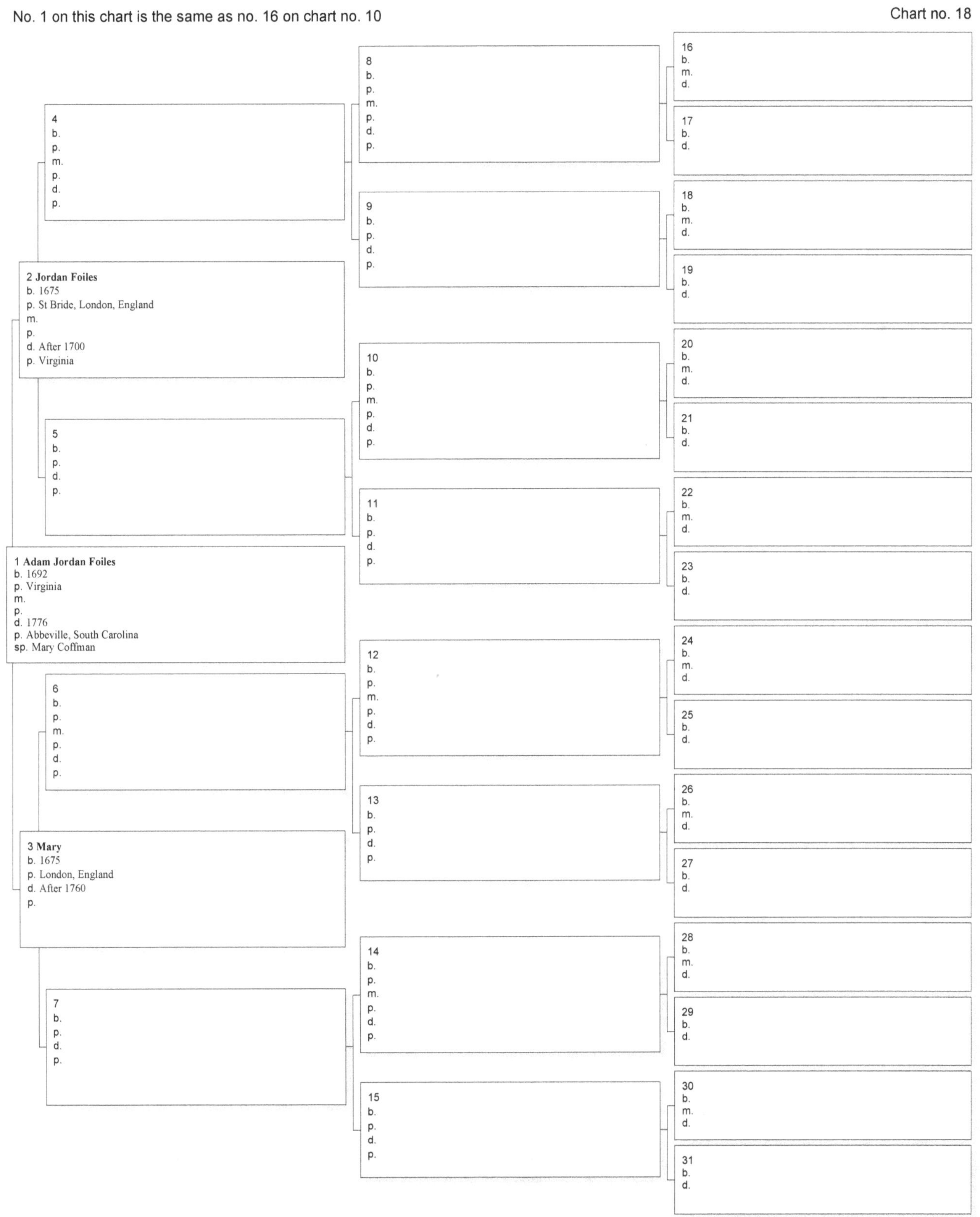

First Generation

1. Philipp Andreass Benz.

> General Notes: Medieval Austria is the ancient homeland of the Benz family. Austria , which was
> originally home to a Celtic people, was conquered by the Roman Empire in about 15 BC Following the
> fall of Rome, Austria was repeatedly invaded by barbarian tribes, such as the Vandals, Visigoths , and
> Huns, who swept in from the east. During the 5th and 6th centuries, the Alemanni, Avars and Slavs settled
> Austria . The Avars were defeated in 785 by the Frankish Emperor Charlemagne , who set
> up the East Mark, which later became known as the Österreich. Austria was ruled by the abenburger
> dynasty until 1278,
> when they were succeeded by the Hapsburg dynasty, which ruled Austria until the 20th century.
> Benz Early Origins The surname Benz was first found in Austria , where the name was closely identified
> in early mediaeval times with the feudal society which would become prominent throughout European
> history. The name would later emerge as a noble family with great influence, having many distinguished branches, and become
> noted for its involvement in social,
> economic and political affairs.
> Benz Spelling Variations One can encounter great variation in the spelling of surnames: in early times, spelling in general, and
> thus the spelling of names was not yet standardized; and later, spellings would change with branching and movement of
> families. Variations of the name Benz include Benz, Benns, Bennze, Benze, Bennse, Bense, Bensz and others.
> Benz Early Notables (pre 1700) Another 42 words (3 lines of text) are included under the topic Early Benz Notables in all our
> The Great Migration Austria was made a republic after the First World War. The Austro-Hungarian Empire was broken up by
> the Treaty of Versailles and many of its people found themselves in the new nation of Czechoslovakia. Many other Austrians
> made their way to North America in the 20th century. Most landed in Philadelphia, later continuing on to the states of Ohio,
> Texas, Illinois, California, New York, and Maryland. Some Austrian settlers also went to western Canada and Ontario.
> Research into the origins of individual families in North America revealed records of the immigration of a number of people
> bearing the name Benz or a variant listed above:
> Benz Settlers in United States in the 18th Century
> Johanes Benz, who arrived in Philadelphia in 1732
> Verena Benz, who setted in Carolina in 1734
> Verena Benz, who arrived in America in 1734

Philipp married **Anna Maria**.

> The child from this marriage was:
> + 2 M   i.   **Johann Philipp Andreae Benz** was born on 24 Jun 1767, was christened on 25 Jun 1767 in EVANGELISCH,
>   SENNFELD, MOSBACH, BADEN, and died on 7 Jan 1803 in Baden, Germany at age 35.

Second Generation (Children)

2. Johann Philipp Andreae Benz *(Philipp Andreass [1])* was born on 24 Jun 1767, was christened on 25 Jun 1767 in EVANGELISCH,
SENNFELD, MOSBACH, BADEN, and died on 7 Jan 1803 in Baden, Germany at age 35.

> General Notes: Record From Deutschland Tote und Beerdigungen, 1582-1958 Was a Shop Keeper

Johann married **Mariae Annae**.

> The child from this marriage was:
> + 3 M   i.   **Mathias Benz** was born on 24 Feb 1785 in Offenburg, Ortenaukreis, Baden-Wuerttemberg, Germany, was
>   christened on 23 Jul 1790, and died on 21 Nov 1873 in Augsburg, Bayern, Germany at age 88.

Third Generation (Grandchildren)

3. Mathias Benz *(Johann Philipp Andreae [2], Philipp Andreass [1])* was born on 24 Feb 1785 in Offenburg, Ortenaukreis, Baden-
Wuerttemberg, Germany, was christened on 23 Jul 1790, and died on 21 Nov 1873 in Augsburg, Bayern, Germany at age 88.

> Mathias married **Ursula Kammerer,** daughter of **Joanne Kammerer** and **Maria Catharina Schmitt,** on 21 Sep 1806 in
> Evangelisch, Gerstetten, Jagstkreis, Wuerttemberg. Ursula was christened on 23 Jul 1790 in KATHOLISCH, HEILIGENSTEIN,
> PFALZ, BAVARIA and died on 20 May 1825 in Greifenberg, Greifenberg, Pommern, Preußen, Deutschland at age 34.

The child from this marriage was:

+ 4   M   i.   **Marcus Benz** was born in 1807 in Baden-Wuerttemberg, Germany and died in 1870 in Calhoun County, Illinois at age 63.

Fourth Generation (Great-Grandchildren)

4. Marcus Benz *(Mathias [3], Johann Philipp Andreae [2], Philipp Andreass [1])* was born in 1807 in Baden-Wuerttemberg, Germany and died in 1870 in Calhoun County, Illinois at age 63.

Marcus married **Kreszentia Schwarz**, daughter of **Sebastian Schwarz** and **Justina Denzler**. Kreszentia was born in 1793 in Baden-Wuerttemberg, Germany, was christened on 19 May 1793, and died in 1852 in Baden-Wuerttemberg, Germany at age 59.

Children from this marriage were:

5   M   i.   **Johann Bapt. Benz** was born on 26 Apr 1832 in Bräunlingen, Schwarzwald-Baar-Kreis, Baden-Wuerttemberg, Germany and died on 27 Sep 1923 in Calhoun County, Illinois at age 91.

6   M   ii. **Charles Dominic Benz** was born on 9 Aug 1833 in Bräunlingen, Baden, Germany and died on 27 Jun 1897 in Carlin, Calhoun County, Illinois at age 63.

+ 7   M   iii. **Martin Benz** was born on 9 Nov 1835 in Bräunlingen, Baden, Germany, died on 15 Aug 1907 in Calhoun County, Illinois at age 71, and was buried in Summit Grove Cemetery.

Fifth Generation (Great Great-Grandchildren)

7. Martin Benz *(Marcus [4], Mathias [3], Johann Philipp Andreae [2], Philipp Andreass [1])* was born on 9 Nov 1835 in Bräunlingen, Baden, Germany, died on 15 Aug 1907 in Calhoun County, Illinois at age 71, and was buried in Summit Grove Cemetery.

General Notes: Name: Martin Benz
Side: Union
Regiment State/Origin: Illinois
Regiment: 12th Regiment, Illinois Cavalry
Company: F&S
Rank In: Sergeant/Saddler
Rank Out: Sergeant/Saddler
Film Number: M539 roll 6

Martin married **Mary Matilda Becker,** daughter of **Jacob (Jakob) Frederick Becker** and **Caroline Sleeper,** on 23 Mar 1866 in Calhoun County, Illinois. Mary was born on 17 Feb 1850 in Shelby County, Tennessee, died on 3 Jan 1917 in Kampsville, Calhoun County, Illinois at age 66, and was buried in Summit Grove Cemetery.

Marriage Notes: Name: Martin Bentz
Gender: Male
Spouse Name: Matilda Becker
Marriage Date: 23 Mar 1866
Marriage County: Calhoun
Comments: This record can be found at the County Court Records, Film # 1305044 - 1305045.

Children from this marriage were:

8   F   i.   **Louisa Wilhemina Benz** was born on 11 Jan 1867 in Kampsville, Calhoun County, Illinois, died on 28 Aug 1943 in Los Angeles County, California at age 76, and was buried in Summit Grove Cemetery.

General Notes: Louisa, daughter of Martin Benz and Mary Matilda Becker. Married Turner Ruyle, son of William Henry Ruyle and Lydia Lumley, 26 September 1888 Calhoun Co., IL. To union were born: Printha Lillian, Roy Robert, Lesly Truman, Hubert Martin, Marvin Dominick and Thelma Hildegard.

9   F   ii. **Theresa Elizabeth Benz** was born on 24 Sep 1868 in Calhoun County, Illinois, died on 18 Oct 1926 in Calhoun County, Illinois at age 58, and was buried in Summit Grove Cemetery.

Theresa married **Joseph Waldheuser**. Joseph was born on 15 Oct 1865 in Calhoun County, Illinois, died on 6 Apr 1934 in Calhoun County, Illinois at age 68, and was buried in Summit Grove Cemetery.

+ 10   M   iii. **Charles Frederick Benz** was born on 24 Nov 1870 in Calhoun County, Illinois, died on 26 Jul 1955 in Kampsville, Calhoun County, Illinois at age 84, and was buried in Summit Grove Cemetery.

11 F iv. **Emma E. Benz** was born on 15 Sep 1875 in Silver Creek, Calhoun County, Illinois and died on 28 Jun 1963 in Columbus, Lowndes County, Mississippi at age 87.

12 F v. **Amanda I. Benz** was born on 12 Jul 1877 in Silver Creek, Calhoun County, Illinois and died in Carrollton, Greene County, Illinois.

13 M vi. **George Robert Benz** was born on 3 Oct 1879 in Silver Creek, Calhoun County, Illinois and died on 23 Aug 1957 in El Paso, El Paso County, Texas at age 77.

14 M vii. **Frank Edward Benz** was born on 12 Jun 1882 in Silver Creek, Calhoun County, Illinois and died on 18 Jan 1904 in El Reno, Canadian County, Oklahoma at age 21.

15 M viii. **William Otto Benz** was born on 21 Jan 1885 in Calhoun County, Illinois, died on 8 Feb 1910 in Anti Nicotine Hosp, St Louis, Missouri at age 25, and was buried in Summit Grove Cemetery.

Sixth Generation (3rd Great-Grandchildren)

10. Charles Frederick Benz *(Martin [5], Marcus [4], Mathias [3], Johann Philipp Andreae [2], Philipp Andreass [1])* was born on 24 Nov 1870 in Calhoun County, Illinois, died on 26 Jul 1955 in Kampsville, Calhoun County, Illinois at age 84, and was buried in Summit Grove Cemetery.

Charles Benz

Charles married **Amanda Elizabeth Foiles,** daughter of **Daniel Webster Foiles** and **Sarah Jane Wiegand,** on 26 Nov 1896 in Calhoun County, Illinois. Amanda was born on 14 Aug 1873 in Hamburg, Calhoun County, Illinois, died on 15 Sep 1960 in Calhoun County, Illinois at age 87, and was buried in Summit Grove Cemetery.

Marriage Notes: At Summit Grove Church

Amanda (Foiles) Benz

Children from this marriage were:

+ 16 M i. **Erwin Alfred Benz** was born on 11 Nov 1897 in Calhoun County, Illinois and died on 26 Dec 1967 in Humboldt, California at age 70.

17 F ii. **Evadna Irene Benz** was born on 3 Sep 1899 in Calhoun County, Illinois, died on 13 Jun 2001 in Calhoun County, Illinois at age 101, and was buried in Summit Grove Cemetery.

Evadna married **Robert Guy Ball**. Robert was born on 12 Sep 1903, died on 21 Apr 1982 in Calhoun County, Illinois at age 78, and was buried in Summit Grove Cemetery.

Evadna Irene Benz

+ 18 M iii. **Alvn Willis "Hap" Benz** was born on 13 Feb 1901 in Calhoun County, Illinois, died on 20 Apr 1988 in Alton,

Madison County, Illinois at age 87, and was buried in Valhalla Cemetery.

+ 19 F iv. **Wilma Mildred Benz** was born on 9 Sep 1903 in Calhoun County, Illinois, died on 20 Jun 1997 in Brighton, Macoupin County, Illinois at age 93, and was buried in Brighton City Cemetery.

+ 20 F v. **Myrtle Marie Benz** was born on 15 Mar 1906 in Caddo County, Illinois, died on 18 Jun 2005 in Jerseyville, Jersey County, Illinois at age 99, and was buried in Oak Grove Cemetery.

+ 21 F vi. **Eula Maurine Benz** was born on 2 Sep 1908 in Calhoun County, Illinois and died on 23 Mar 1994 at age 85.

+ 22 M vii. **Dean Howard Benz** was born on 14 Feb 1911 in Calhoun County, Illinois, died on 22 Jan 1999 in Brighton, Macoupin County, Illinois at age 87, and was buried in Brighton City Cemetery.

+ 23 F viii. **Mary Jane Benz** was born on 19 Jun 1914 in Calhoun County, Illinois and died on 27 May 2002 in Sarasota, Manatee, Florida at age 87.

+ 24 F ix. **Wanda Lucille Benz** was born on 21 Nov 1918 in Calhoun County, Illinois, died on 5 Aug 2008 in East Peoria, Tazewell County, Illinois at age 89, and was buried in Valhalla Cemetery.

Seventh Generation (4th Great-Grandchildren)

16. Erwin Alfred Benz *(Charles Frederick [6], Martin [5], Marcus [4], Mathias [3], Johann Philipp Andreae [2], Philipp Andreass [1])* was born on 11 Nov 1897 in Calhoun County, Illinois and died on 26 Dec 1967 in Humboldt, California at age 70.

Erwin married **Edith M. Rulon**. Edith was born on 30 Sep 1900 in Calhoun County, Illinois, died on 10 Jan 1948 in Calhoun County, Illinois at age 47, and was buried in Fox Creek Cemetery.

The child from this marriage was:

25 F i. **Wauneta L "Juanita" Benz** was born on 3 Dec 1923 in East Alton, Illinois, died on 13 Nov 1993 in Hamburg, Calhoun County, Illinois at age 69, and was buried in Fox Creek Cemetery.

18. Alvn Willis "Hap" Benz *(Charles Frederick [6], Martin [5], Marcus [4], Mathias [3], Johann Philipp Andreae [2], Philipp Andreass [1])* was born on 13 Feb 1901 in Calhoun County, Illinois, died on 20 Apr 1988 in Alton, Madison County, Illinois at age 87, and was buried in Valhalla Cemetery.

Alvn married **Jewell Mae Battershell** in 1923 in Illinois. Jewell was born on 19 Sep 1903 in Madison County, Illinois and died on 22 Mar 1947 in San Francisco, San Francisco County, California at age 43.

Alvn Willis Benz

The child from this marriage was:

+ 26 M i. **Robert LeRoy "Bobby" Benz** was born on 12 Sep 1924 in Calhoun County, Illinois, died on 14 Jan 1975 in Alton, Madison County, Illinois at age 50, and was buried in Oakwood Cemetery.

Alvn next married **Ruth Elizabeth Adams**. Ruth was born on 12 Mar 1912 in Hancock County, Illinois, died in May 1970 in Alton, Madison County, Illinois at age 58, and was buried in Valhalla Cemetery.

19. Wilma Mildred Benz *(Charles Frederick [6], Martin [5], Marcus [4], Mathias [3], Johann Philipp Andreae [2], Philipp Andreass [1])* was born on 9 Sep 1903 in Calhoun County, Illinois, died on 20 Jun 1997 in Brighton, Macoupin County, Illinois at age 93, and was buried in Brighton City Cemetery.

Wilma married **Ralph Haycraft** on 19 Jun 1943 in Rolla, Phelps, Missouri. Ralph was born on 5 Sep 1905 in Saint Louis County, Missouri, died on 25 Apr 1974 in Brighton, Macoupin County, Illinois at age 68, and was buried in Brighton City Cemetery.

Wilma Mildred Benz

The child from this marriage was:

+ 27 F i. **Betty Benz**.

Descendants of Philipp Andreass Benz

20. Myrtle Marie Benz *(Charles Frederick [6], Martin [5], Marcus [4], Mathias [3], Johann Philipp Andreae [2], Philipp Andreass [1])* was born on 15 Mar 1906 in Caddo County, Illinois, died on 18 Jun 2005 in Jerseyville, Jersey County, Illinois at age 99, and was buried in Oak Grove Cemetery.

Myrtle Marie Benz

     General Notes: School Teacher

Myrtle married **Everett James Sweetman**. Everett was born on 27 Jul 1905 in Calhoun County, Illinois, died on 5 Jul 1979 in Jersey County, Illinois at age 73, and was buried in Oak Grove Cemetery.

The child from this marriage was:

\+ 28 F   i. **Virginia Sweetman** was born circa 1932 in Illinois.

21. Eula Maurine Benz *(Charles Frederick [6], Martin [5], Marcus [4], Mathias [3], Johann Philipp Andreae [2], Philipp Andreass [1])* was born on 2 Sep 1908 in Calhoun County, Illinois and died on 23 Mar 1994 at age 85.

Eula Maurine Benz

Eula married **Robert Buress**.

The child from this marriage was:

\+ 29 F   i. **Shirley Benz**.

22. Dean Howard Benz *(Charles Frederick [6], Martin [5], Marcus [4], Mathias [3], Johann Philipp Andreae [2], Philipp Andreass [1])* was born on 14 Feb 1911 in Calhoun County, Illinois, died on 22 Jan 1999 in Brighton, Macoupin County, Illinois at age 87, and was buried in Brighton City Cemetery.

Dean Howard Benz

     General Notes: They have 2 children

Dean married **Marguerite "Maggie"**. Marguerite was born on 18 Nov 1917, died on 23 Oct 1983 in Brighton, Macoupin County, Illinois at age 65, and was buried in Brighton City Cemetery.

Children from this marriage were:

30 M   i. **Fred Benz**.

31 F   ii. **Mary Ann Benz**.

\+ 32 F   iii. **Alice Marie Benz**.

23. Mary Jane Benz *(Charles Frederick [6], Martin [5], Marcus [4], Mathias [3], Johann Philipp Andreae [2], Philipp Andreass [1])* was born on 19 Jun 1914 in Calhoun County, Illinois and died on 27 May 2002 in Sarasota, Manatee, Florida at age 87.

Mary Jane Benz

> General Notes: They have 2 sons

Mary married **Walter Moore**.

Children from this marriage were:

+ 33   M   i.   **Marlin Moore**.

+ 34   M   ii.   **Carlton Moore**.

24. Wanda Lucille Benz *(Charles Frederick [6], Martin [5], Marcus [4], Mathias [3], Johann Philipp Andreae [2], Philipp Andreass [1])* was born on 21 Nov 1918 in Calhoun County, Illinois, died on 5 Aug 2008 in East Peoria, Tazewell County, Illinois at age 89, and was buried in Valhalla Cemetery.

Wanda Benz

> General Notes: Daughter of Charles F. and Amanda Elizabeth Foiles Benz. She married Raymond Roe on June 21, 1946, in Brighton, Ill. He preceded her in death on July 1, 1973, in Hyden, Ky. She later married Melvin Dudley on June 15, 1981, in East Peoria, Ill. He preceded her in death on Sept. 10, 1991, in Peoria.
>
> Surviving are two daughters, Robin (Lee) Benway and; and her grandson, Cody Benway. Linda (Harry) Karle.
>
> She was preceded in death by her parents, five sisters and three brothers.
>
> Wanda was Head cook for the Creve Coeur school district and was the cafeteria manager at Robein Grade School for nine years.

Wanda married **Raymond Keith Roe**, son of **Claude Clifton Roe** and **Cora Bell Sly,** on 15 Jun 1946 in Brighton, Macoupin County, Illinois. Raymond was born on 21 Oct 1917 in Roodhouse, Greene County, Illinois, died on 1 Jul 1973 in Hyden, Leslie County, Kentucky at age 55, and was buried in Valhalla Cemetery.

Raymond Keith Roe

Descendants of Philipp Andreass Benz

Children from this marriage were:

    35 F   i. **Linda Susan Roe** was born on 3 Oct 1948 in Peoria, Tazewell County, Illinois.

General Notes: Nurse Practitioner/ Certified Nurse Midwife for 30 years
Delivered 3100 babies
Retired in 2011

Linda Row Karle

Linda married **Harry Karle** on 25 Feb 1989 in Vernon, Florida. Harry was born on 7 Feb 1950 in Baltimore, Maryland.

Harry Karle

 + 36 F   ii. **Robin Elizabeth Roe** was born on 22 May 1957 in Peoria, Tazewell County, Illinois.

Wanda next married **Melvin Dudley** on 20 Jun 1981 in East Peoria, Tazewell County, Illinois. Melvin was born on 24 Jan 1923 in Peoria, Tazewell County, Illinois and died on 10 Sep 1991 in East Peoria, Tazewell County, Illinois at age 68.

Melvin F. Dudley

Eighth Generation (5th Great-Grandchildren)

26. Robert LeRoy "Bobby" Benz *(Alvn Willis "Hap" [7], Charles Frederick [6], Martin [5], Marcus [4], Mathias [3], Johann Philipp Andreae [2], Philipp Andreass [1])* was born on 12 Sep 1924 in Calhoun County, Illinois, died on 14 Jan 1975 in Alton, Madison County, Illinois at age 50, and was buried in Oakwood Cemetery.

Robert married someone.

His children were:

    37 M   i. **Tommy Benz**.

    38 F   ii. **Debra Benz**.

    39 F   iii. **Cindy Benz**.

27. Betty Benz *(Wilma Mildred Benz [7], Charles Frederick [6], Martin [5], Marcus [4], Mathias [3], Johann Philipp Andreae [2], Philipp Andreass [1])*.

Betty married **John Rain**.

Children from this marriage were:

    40 M   i. **John Rain**.

41   M   ii.   **Dan Rain**.

28. Virginia Sweetman *(Myrtle Marie Benz [7], Charles Frederick [6], Martin [5], Marcus [4], Mathias [3], Johann Philipp Andreae [2], Philipp Andreass [1])* was born circa 1932 in Illinois.

Virginia married **Glenn Thomas**.

Children from this marriage were:
   42   M   i.   **David Thomas**.

   43   M   ii.   **Douglas Thomas**.

   44   M   iii.   **Dennis Thomas**.

29. Shirley Benz *(Eula Maurine Benz [7], Charles Frederick [6], Martin [5], Marcus [4], Mathias [3], Johann Philipp Andreae [2], Philipp Andreass [1])*.

Shirley married **Herschel Mouser**.

Children from this marriage were:
   45   M   i.   **Rodney Mouser**.

   46   M   ii.   **Robert "Bobby" Mouser**.

32. Alice Marie Benz *(Dean Howard [7], Charles Frederick [6], Martin [5], Marcus [4], Mathias [3], Johann Philipp Andreae [2], Philipp Andreass [1])*.

Alice married **Jeff Stone**.

Children from this marriage were:
   47   F   i.   **Jennifer**.

   48   F   ii.   **Jessica**.

33. Marlin Moore *(Mary Jane Benz [7], Charles Frederick [6], Martin [5], Marcus [4], Mathias [3], Johann Philipp Andreae [2], Philipp Andreass [1])*.

Marlin married **Lorraine**.

The child from this marriage was:
   49   F   i.   **Tracy Moore**.

34. Carlton Moore *(Mary Jane Benz [7], Charles Frederick [6], Martin [5], Marcus [4], Mathias [3], Johann Philipp Andreae [2], Philipp Andreass [1])*.

Carlton married **Nancy**.

The child from this marriage was:
   50   M   i.   **Brad Moore**.

36. Robin Elizabeth Roe *(Wanda Lucille Benz [7], Charles Frederick [6], Martin [5], Marcus [4], Mathias [3], Johann Philipp Andreae [2], Philipp Andreass [1])* was born on 22 May 1957 in Peoria, Tazewell County, Illinois.

    General Notes: Teacher for 30 years, retired in 2012

Robin married **Lee Benway** on 24 Dec 1988 in East Peoria, Tazewell County, Illinois. Lee was born on 31 May 1950 in Peoria, Tazewell County, Illinois.

Robin & Lee

The child from this marriage was:

Cody Ray Benway

51 M   i.   **Cody Ray Benway** was born on 18 Aug 1992 in Peoria, Tazewell County, Illinois.

General Notes: SIU, Law School, graduated in 2018

First Generation

52. Sebastian Schwarz, son of **Sebastian Schwarz** and **Maria Anna Baumann,** was christened on 28 Jan 1772 in KATHOLISCH, SINGEN, KONSTANZ, BADEN and died in 1822 at age 50.

> General Notes: Name   Sebastian Schwarz
> Gender   Male
> Christening Date   28 Jan 1772
> Christening Place   KATHOLISCH, SINGEN, KONSTANZ, BADEN
> Death Date   1822
> Father's Name   Sebastian Schwarz
> Mother's Name   Maria Schwarz
> Citing this Record
> "Deutschland Geburten und Taufen, 1558-1898,

Sebastian married **Justina Denzler**, daughter of **Carl Wilhelm Denzler** and **Anna Dorothea**. Justina was christened on 25 Jun 1776 in EVANGELISCH-REFORMIERTE, BAD DUERKHEIM, PFALZ, BAVARIA.

The child from this marriage was:

+ 53   F   i.   **Kreszentia Schwarz** was born in 1793 in Baden-Wuerttemberg, Germany, was christened on 19 May 1793, and died in 1852 in Baden-Wuerttemberg, Germany at age 59.

Second Generation (Children)

53. Kreszentia Schwarz *(Sebastian [1])* was born in 1793 in Baden-Wuerttemberg, Germany, was christened on 19 May 1793, and died in 1852 in Baden-Wuerttemberg, Germany at age 59.

> General Notes: Name   Mar. Crescentia Schwarz
> Gender   Female
> Christening Date   19 May 1793
> Christening Place   Erolzheim, Württemberg, Germany
> Father's Name   Sebastian Schwarz
> Mother's Name   Justina Denzler
> Citing this Record
> "Deutschland Geburten und Taufen, 1558-1898,"

Kreszentia married **Marcus Benz**, son of **Mathias Benz** and **Ursula Kammerer**. Marcus was born in 1807 in Baden-Wuerttemberg, Germany and died in 1870 in Calhoun County, Illinois at age 63.

(Duplicate Line. See Person 4 on Page 20)

First Generation

54. Christopher Becker.

Christopher married **Agnes**.

The child from this marriage was:
+ 55 M   i. **Jean Jacques Becker** was born on 15 Dec 1799 in Schwegenheim, Bayern, Germany and died on 23 Apr 1841 in Ahsen, Westfalen, Preußen, Germany at age 41.

Second Generation (Children)

55. Jean Jacques Becker *(Christopher ¹)* was born on 15 Dec 1799 in Schwegenheim, Bayern, Germany and died on 23 Apr 1841 in Ahsen, Westfalen, Preußen, Germany at age 41.

General Notes: Name   J. Jacob Becker
Event Date   1799
Gender   Male
Birth Date   15 Dec 1799
Birth Year   1799
Christening Date   16 Dec 1799
Christening Place Schwegenheim, Bayern, Germany
Father's Name   Christoph Becker
Mother's Name   Agnes
Citing this Record
"Deutschland Geburten und Taufen, 1558-1898," database, FamilySearch

Name   Joseph Becker
Gender   Male
Burial Date   26 Apr 1841
Death Date   23 Apr 1841
Death Place   Ahsen, Westfalen, Preußen, Germany
Age   58
Birth Date   1783
Marital Status   Widowed
Citing this Record
"Deutschland Tote und Beerdigungen, 1582-1958," database, FamilySearch

Jean married **Caroline Reinhardt,** daughter of **Peter Reinhardt** and **Apollonia Narz,** on 21 Dec 1814 in KUSEL, PFALZ, BAVARIA. Caroline was born on 25 Jan 1780 in Holzhausen (vor der Höhe), Hessen, Germany and died on 14 Apr 1819 in Kusel (Ba. Kusel), Bayern, Germany at age 39.

The child from this marriage was:
+ 56 M   i. **Jacob (Jakob) Frederick Becker** was born on 25 Dec 1815 in Baden, Germany, was christened on 26 Dec 1815 in KUSEL, PFALZ, BAVARIA, and died on 12 Jun 1863 in Calhoun County, Illinois at age 47.

Third Generation (Grandchildren)

56. Jacob (Jakob) Frederick Becker *(Jean Jacques ², Christopher ¹)* was born on 25 Dec 1815 in Baden, Germany, was christened on 26 Dec 1815 in KUSEL, PFALZ, BAVARIA, and died on 12 Jun 1863 in Calhoun County, Illinois at age 47.

General Notes: Name   Friedrich Jacob Becker
Gender   Male
Christening Date   01 Jan 1816
Christening Place EVANGELISCH,KUSEL,PFALZ,BAVARIA
Father's Name   Jacob Becker
Mother's Name   Caroline Reinhardt
Citing this Record
"Deutschland Geburten und Taufen, 1558-1898," database, FamilySearch

Jacob married **Caroline Sleeper,** daughter of **Johann Jobst Schlepper** and **Wilhelmine Sophie Cathar. Meiers,** in 1849. Caroline was born on 9 Mar 1821 in Horne, Lippe, Germany and died in 1881 in Carlin, Calhoun County, Illinois at age 60.

The child from this marriage was:
+ 57 F   i. **Mary Matilda Becker** was born on 17 Feb 1850 in Shelby County, Tennessee, died on 3 Jan 1917 in Kampsville, Calhoun County, Illinois at age 66, and was buried in Summit Grove Cemetery.

Fourth Generation (Great-Grandchildren)

57. Mary Matilda Becker *(Jacob (Jakob) Frederick [3], Jean Jacques [2], Christopher [1])* was born on 17 Feb 1850 in Shelby County, Tennessee, died on 3 Jan 1917 in Kampsville, Calhoun County, Illinois at age 66, and was buried in Summit Grove Cemetery.

General Notes: OBITUARY: Mary Matilda Becker was born at Memphis, Tenn. February, 17, 1850. She came to this country when about eleven years old and spent most of her life in this County, except for a few years she spent in Oklahoma. On March 3, 1866, she was united in marriage to Martin Benz at Silver Creek, Ill. This union was blessed with four sons and four daughters. Frank E. and Will O. Benz have died earlier. The other children are Charles F. Benz of Hinton, Okla.; Geo. R. Benz of Kenna, New Mexico; Louisa W., wife of Turner Ruyle and Theresa, wife of Joseph Waldheuser, both of near Kampsville, Ill.; Emma, wife of W. A. Jackson of Mobile, Alabama; and Amanda, wife of Richard Williams, Carrollton, Ill. Her husband preceded her in death August 15, 1907. She died January 3, 1917 at her daughter's home, Mrs. Joseph Waldheuser, where she has been living the last few years. Two surviving sons, four daughters and 21 grand children. Funeral services at Presbyterian Church in Kampsville, Ill., Summit Grove Cemetery. Earl W. Barrett, Pastor of the M. E. Church, Hamburg, Ill. (Unknown Calhoun County newspaper; Jan 1917)

Mary married **Martin Benz,** son of **Marcus Benz** and **Kreszentia Schwarz,** on 23 Mar 1866 in Calhoun County, Illinois. Martin was born on 9 Nov 1835 in Bräunlingen, Baden, Germany, died on 15 Aug 1907 in Calhoun County, Illinois at age 71, and was buried in Summit Grove Cemetery.

Marriage Notes: Name: Martin Bentz
Gender: Male
Spouse Name: Matilda Becker
Marriage Date: 23 Mar 1866
Marriage County: Calhoun
Comments: This record can be found at the County Court Records, Film # 1305044 - 1305045.

(Duplicate Line. See Person 7 on Page 20)

Descendants of Samuel Schlepper

First Generation

58. Samuel Schlepper.

Samuel married **Catarina Margaretha Elbertshagen**.

The child from this marriage was:
+ 59 M   i. **Johann Jobst Schlepper** was born on 20 Dec 1778 in Remscheid, Rheinland, Preußen, Germany and died on 14 Mar 1847 in Hellinghausen, Westfalen, Preußen, Germany at age 68.

Second Generation (Children)

59. Johann Jobst Schlepper *(Samuel [1])* was born on 20 Dec 1778 in Remscheid, Rheinland, Preußen, Germany and died on 14 Mar 1847 in Hellinghausen, Westfalen, Preußen, Germany at age 68.

> General Notes: Name   Johann Wilhelm Helmig Schlieper
> Gender   Male
> Burial Date   17 Mar 1847
> Death Date   14 Mar 1847
> Death Place   Hellinghausen, Westfalen, Preußen, Germany
> Age   74
> Birth Date   1773
> Marital Status   Married

Johann married **Wilhelmine Sophie Cathar. Meiers,** daughter of **Anton Henrich Meiers** and **Wilhelmine Elisabeth,** on 23 Aug 1801 in Horne, Lippe, Germany. Wilhelmine was born on 18 Feb 1791 in Horne, Lippe, Germany and died on 17 May 1827 in Horne, Lippe, Germany at age 36.

> Marriage Notes: Name   Jobst Hermann Schlepper
> Spouse's Name   Wilhelmine Sophie Cathar. Meiers
> Event Date   23 Aug 1801
> Event Place   Detmold, Evangelisch, Lippe, Germ
> Citing this Record
> "Deutschland Heiraten, 1558-1929," database, FamilySearch

Children from this marriage were:
   60 F   i. **Amalia Wilhelmine Schlepper** was christened on 27 Oct 1819 in Horne, Lippe, Germany and died on 27 Sep 1821 in Horne, Lippe, Germany at age 1.

+ 61 F   ii. **Caroline Sleeper** was born on 9 Mar 1821 in Horne, Lippe, Germany and died in 1881 in Carlin, Calhoun County, Illinois at age 60.

   62 M   iii. **Simon August Schlepper** was christened on 5 Nov 1826 in Horne, Lippe, Germany.

Third Generation (Grandchildren)

61. Caroline Sleeper *(Johann Jobst [2], Samuel [1])* was born on 9 Mar 1821 in Horne, Lippe, Germany and died in 1881 in Carlin, Calhoun County, Illinois at age 60.

> General Notes: Name   Karoline Luise Schlepper
> Gender   Female
> Birthplace   Horn, , , Germany
> Father's Name   Johann Jobst Schlepper
> Mother's Name   Wilhelmine Schlepper
> Citing this Record
> "Deutschland Geburten und Taufen, 1558-1898," database, FamilySearch

Caroline married **Jacob (Jakob) Frederick Becker,** son of **Jean Jacques Becker** and **Caroline Reinhardt,** in 1849. Jacob was born on 25 Dec 1815 in Baden, Germany, was christened on 26 Dec 1815 in KUSEL, PFALZ, BAVARIA, and died on 12 Jun 1863 in Calhoun County, Illinois at age 47.

(Duplicate Line. See Person 56 on Page 29)

Descendants of Adam Jordan Foiles

First Generation

63. Adam Jordan Foiles, son of **Jordan Foiles** and **Mary,** was born in 1692 in Virginia and died in 1776 in Abbeville, South Carolina at age 84.

Adam married **Mary Coffman**. Mary was born in 1692 and died in 1750 in Augusta County, Virginia at age 58.

The child from this marriage was:
+ 64 M   i.   **Robert Foiles** was born in 1715 in Virginia and died in Jan 1753 in Pocahontas County, Virginia at age 38.

Second Generation (Children)

64. Robert Foiles *(Adam Jordan [1])* was born in 1715 in Virginia and died in Jan 1753 in Pocahontas County, Virginia at age 38.

Robert married **Elizabeth Tygart** in 1737 in Augusta County, Virginia. Elizabeth was born in 1717 in Virginia and died in Jan 1753 in Pocahontas County, Virginia at age 36.

Children from this marriage were:
+ 65 M   i.   **Captain John Adam Foiles Sr** was born in 1738 in Spotsylvania County, Virginia and died on 17 Jan 1781 in Pendleton, Anderson County, South Carolina, at age 43.

   66 M   ii.   **Child Foiles**.

Third Generation (Grandchildren)

65. Captain John Adam Foiles Sr *(Robert [2], Adam Jordan [1])* was born in 1738 in Spotsylvania County, Virginia and died on 17 Jan 1781 in Pendleton, Anderson County, South Carolina, at age 43.

John married **Mary Catherine**. Mary was born in 1738 in Virginia and died on 16 Dec 1816 in Cowpens, Spartanburg County, South Carolina at age 78.

The child from this marriage was:
+ 67 M   i.   **John Foiles Jr** was born on 31 Mar 1760 in Augusta County, Virginia, died on 1 Oct 1834 in Burnt Prairie, Wayne, Illinois at age 74, and was buried in Liberty Cemetery.

Fourth Generation (Great-Grandchildren)

67. John Foiles Jr *(John Adam Sr (Captain) [3], Robert [2], Adam Jordan [1])* was born on 31 Mar 1760 in Augusta County, Virginia, died on 1 Oct 1834 in Burnt Prairie, Wayne, Illinois at age 74, and was buried in Liberty Cemetery.

John Files Revolutionary War Marker

John married **Ann Eddy** on 10 Nov 1781 in Rutherford County, North Carolina. Ann died in 1786 in Greeneville County, South Carolina.

Children from this marriage were:
   68 M   i.   **William Foiles** was born in 1784 in Greeneville County, South Carolina and died on 14 Jul 1855 in Mill Shoals White County, Illinois at age 71.

+ 69 M   ii.   **John F. Foiles** was born on 23 Dec 1785 in Cecil County, Maryland and died on 7 May 1870 in Kampsville, Calhoun, Illinois at age 84.

   70 M   iii.   **Thomas Foiles** was born in 1788 and died in 1848 at age 60.

Fifth Generation (Great Great-Grandchildren)

69. John F. Foiles *(John Jr [4], John Adam Sr (Captain) [3], Robert [2], Adam Jordan [1])* was born on 23 Dec 1785 in Cecil County, Maryland and died on 7 May 1870 in Kampsville, Calhoun, Illinois at age 84.

John married **Margaret Peggy Hovermale,** daughter of **John Christian Hovermale** and **Mary Magdaline,** on 13 Apr 1810 in Berkeley County, Virginia. Margaret was born in 1789 in Virginia and died in 1835 in Cabell County, Virginia at age 46.

Grave of John Foiles

Children from this marriage were:

71 F   i.   **Elizabeth Foiles** was born in 1810 in Jefferson, Alexandria, Virginia and died on 5 Apr 1891 in Calhoun County, Illinois at age 81.

72 M   ii.   **James Foiles** was born on 18 Oct 1811 in Jefferson, Alexandria, Virginia and died on 17 Feb 1891 in Calhoun County, Illinois at age 79.

+ 73 M   iii.   **Joseph Foiles** was born on 20 Jun 1813 in Frederick County, Virginia, died on 31 Jan 1911 in Kampsville, Calhoun County, Illinois at age 97, and was buried in Summit Grove Cemetery.

74 M   iv.   **Daniel Foiles** was born in 1815 in Jefferson, Alexandria, Virginia and died in 1816 in Jefferson, Alexandria, Virginia at age 1.

75 M   v.   **John B. Foiles** was born in May 1817 in Jefferson, Alexandria, Virginia and died on 2 Dec 1921 in Calhoun County, Illinois at age 104.

76 M   vi.   **Daniel Foiles** was born in 1819 in Jefferson, Alexandria, Virginia and died on 12 Apr 1894 in Moniteau, Missouri at age 75.

77 M   vii.   **Benjamin Foiles** was born about 1820 in Jefferson, Culpeper, Virginia and died in 1900 in Calhoun County, Illinois about age 80.

78 F   viii.   **Mary Foiles** was born in 1820 in Jefferson, Alexandria, Virginia and died in 1868 in Lawrence County, Ohio at age 48.

79 F   ix.   **Sarah Foiles** was born circa 1820 in Jefferson, Alexandria, Virginia.

80 M   x.   **Frederic Isaiah Foiles** was born on 13 Feb 1824 in Jefferson, Culpeper County, Virginia and died on 29 Dec 1902 in Calhoun County, Illinois at age 78.

81 F   xi.   **Eleanor Foiles** was born on 27 Jun 1826 in Jefferson, Alexandria, Virginia and died on 6 Feb 1871 in Bellelview, Calhoun County, Illinois at age 44.

82 F   xii.   **Amanda Foiles** was born in 1827 in Jefferson, Alexandria, Virginia and died on 25 Apr 1902 in California, Moniteau, Missouri at age 75.

83 F   xiii.   **Jeptha Foiles** was born in 1828 in Jefferson, Alexandria, Virginia.

84 M   xiv.   **Henry Vinson Foiles** was born on 1 Mar 1829 in Cabell County, Virginia and died on 12 Jan 1884 in Belleview, Calhoun County, Illinois at age 54.

85 M   xv.   **Thomas J. Foiles** was born in 1830 in Cabell County, Virginia and died in 1850 in Calhoun County, Illinois at age 20.

86 F   xvi.   **Margaret Ann Foiles** was born in 1833 in Jefferson, Alexandria, Virginia and died on 17 Nov 1888 at age 55.

87 F   xvii.   **Mahala Jane D. Foiles** was born about 1836 in Virginia.

88 M xviii.   **Timothy Lewis Foiles** was born on 20 Dec 1841 in Lawrence County, Ohio and died on 28 Jun 1912 in Kampsville, Calhoun County, Illinois at age 70.

Descendants of Adam Jordan Foiles

Sixth Generation (3rd Great-Grandchildren)

73. Joseph Foiles *(John F. [5], John Jr [4], John Adam Sr (Captain) [3], Robert [2], Adam Jordan [1])* was born on 20 Jun 1813 in Frederick County, Virginia, died on 31 Jan 1911 in Kampsville, Calhoun County, Illinois at age 97, and was buried in Summit Grove Cemetery.

Joseph married **Hannah Ansell,** daughter of **Melchor Ansell** and **Elizabeth Wentz,** on 5 Mar 1835 in Cabell County, Virginia. Hannah was born on 1 May 1814 in Virginia, died on 23 Apr 1882 in Kampsville, Calhoun County, Illinois at age 67, and was buried in Summit Grove Cemetery.

Hannah Ansell Foiles

Children from this marriage were:

    89   F   i.   **Sarah Foiles** was born about 1838 in Cabell County, Virginia.

    90   F   ii.   **Jacob Foiles** was born about 1839 in Cabell County, Virginia.

+ 91   M   iii.   **Daniel Webster Foiles** was born on 9 Jan 1843 in Cabell County, Virginia, died on 6 Sep 1933 in Kampsville, Calhoun County, Illinois at age 90, and was buried in Summit Grove Cemetery.

    92   F   iv.   **Amanda Ann Foiles** was born about 1846 in Cabell County, Virginia.

    93   F   v.   **Emily Foiles** was born about 1848 in Cabell County, Virginia.

    94   F   vi.   **Virginia Foiles** was born about 1850 in Cabell County, Virginia.

    95   F   vii.   **Mary Foiles** was born about 1852 in Cabell County, Virginia.

    96   M viii.   **Albert Foiles** was born about 1854 in Cabell County, Virginia.

    97   F   ix.   **America Foiles** was born about 1857 in Calhoun County, Illinois.

Seventh Generation (4th Great-Grandchildren)

91. Daniel Webster Foiles *(Joseph [6], John F. [5], John Jr [4], John Adam Sr (Captain) [3], Robert [2], Adam Jordan [1])* was born on 9 Jan 1843 in Cabell County, Virginia, died on 6 Sep 1933 in Kampsville, Calhoun County, Illinois at age 90, and was buried in Summit Grove Cemetery.

Daniel Webster Foiles

General Notes: Daniel W. Foiles -- Obituary.

Daniel W. Foiles was born in Cabel County, Virginia now West Virginia, Jan 9, 1843. He came to Calhoun County with his parents in pioneer days, at the age of 13 years. He grew to manhood on the old homestead. Later purchaced the farm on which he lived for 61 years. October 27, 1872. he was united in marriage with Sarah J. Wiegand, to this union was born five children, Four survive him. The wife and one son, Lafayatte, having preceded him to his grave. He is survived by one daughter, Mrs. Amanda Benz of Kampsville and three sons, Charles of Belleview, Oscar of Raymond S.D. , and Dennis of Gilead; also three sisters, eighteen grandchildren and 5 great grandchildren, many other relitives and a host of friends. He was converted and joined the Methodist church about fifty years ago, and remained a good and faithful servant until the Master called for him on Sept. 6, 1933. at the age of 91 years, 7 months, and 28 days. "Servant of God, well done, Thy glorious warefare's past, The battle's fought, the race is won, And thou art crowned at Last." Funeral Services was conduted Saturday afternoon at the Summit Grove Tabernacle by the Rev. J. P. Suhling. Intermant was in the Summit Grove Cemetery.

Daniel married **Sarah Jane Wiegand,** daughter of **Henry Wiegand** and **Martha Emma Tischer,** on 27 Oct 1872 in Calhoun County, Illinois. Sarah was born on 13 Sep 1853 in Calhoun County, Illinois, died on 18 Jan 1926 in Kampsville, Calhoun County, Illinois at age 72, and was buried in Summit Grove Cemetery.

Sarah Jane Wiegand
Foiles

> Marriage Notes: Name: Daniel W Foiles
> Gender: Male
> Spouse Name: Sarah J Wiegand
> Marriage Date: 27 Oct 1872
> Marriage County: Calhoun
> Comments: This record can be found at the County Court Records, Film # 1305044 - 1305045.

Children from this marriage were:

+ 98   F   i.   **Amanda Elizabeth Foiles** was born on 14 Aug 1873 in Hamburg, Calhoun County, Illinois, died on 15 Sep 1960 in Calhoun County, Illinois at age 87, and was buried in Summit Grove Cemetery.

+ 99   M   ii.   **Charles Henry Foiles** was born on 3 Nov 1875 in Calhoun County, Illinois, died on 29 Dec 1945 in Belleview, Calhoun County, Illinois at age 70, and was buried in Summit Grove Cemetery.

+ 100   M   iii.   **Joseph Oscar Foiles** was born on 29 Dec 1877 in Calhoun County, Illinois, died in Jun 1969 in Raymond, Clark County, South Dakota at age 91, and was buried in Rose Hill Cemetery.

  101   M   iv.   **Philip Lafayette Foiles** was born on 28 Jun 1886 in Calhoun County, Illinois, died on 26 Jul 1917 in Kampsville, Calhoun County, Illinois at age 31, and was buried in Summit Grove Cemetery.

+ 102   M   v.   **Dennis Wilber Foiles** was born on 8 Feb 1888 in Calhoun County, Illinois, died in Jul 1968 in Calhoun County, Illinois at age 80, and was buried in Hardin Cemetery.

Eighth Generation (5th Great-Grandchildren)

98. Amanda Elizabeth Foiles *(Daniel Webster [7], Joseph [6], John F. [5], John Jr [4], John Adam Sr (Captain) [3], Robert [2], Adam Jordan [1])* was born on 14 Aug 1873 in Hamburg, Calhoun County, Illinois, died on 15 Sep 1960 in Calhoun County, Illinois at age 87, and was buried in Summit Grove Cemetery.

> General Notes: Alton Evening Telegraph (Alton, Illinois) 7 September 1960 Wednesday. Page 20
> Mrs. Amanda Benz Rites Set Thursday Died of a Stroke
>
> Funeral rites for Mrs. Amanda Benz of Kampsville will be conducted Thursday at 2 PM in the Church of Nazarene, Summit Groves, Calhoun County, instead of today as was incorrectly listed in the announcement of the death.
> The body is at C.C. Hanks Funeral Home, Hardin, where friends may call at 2 PM today and until noon Thursday when the body will be moved to the church.
> Mrs. Benz, who died Monday in Wood River Township Hospital, is survived by six daughters,
> Mrs Evadna Ball of Roxana; Mrs. Wilma Haycraft of Brighton; Mrs. Myrtle Sweetman, Jerseyville; Mrs. Eula Burress, Alton; Mrs. Mary Jane Moore, New Boston, Ohio, and Mrs. Wanda Roe, of Creve Coeur: three sons, Irwin of Quincy, California; Alva of Alton, and Dean of Brighton; 13 grandchildren, and 10 great-grandchildren.

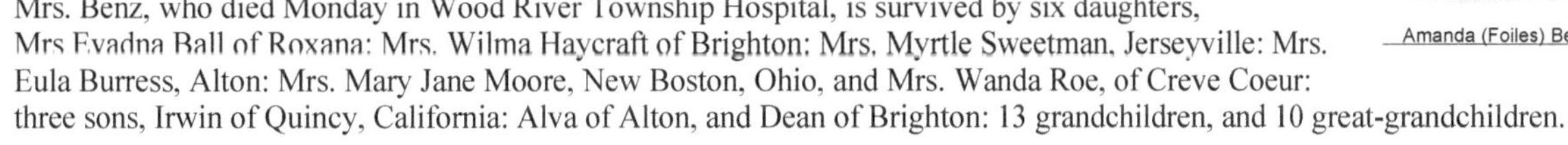

Amanda (Foiles) Benz

Amanda married **Charles Frederick Benz,** son of **Martin Benz** and **Mary Matilda Becker,** on 26 Nov 1896 in Calhoun County, Illinois. Charles was born on 24 Nov 1870 in Calhoun County, Illinois, died on 26 Jul 1955 in Kampsville, Calhoun County, Illinois at age 84, and was buried in Summit Grove Cemetery.

> Marriage Notes: At Summit Grove Church

(Duplicate Line. See Person 10 on Page 21)

Charles Benz

99. Charles Henry Foiles *(Daniel Webster [7], Joseph [6], John F. [5], John Jr [4], John Adam Sr (Captain) [3], Robert [2], Adam Jordan [1])* was born on 3 Nov 1875 in Calhoun County, Illinois, died on 29 Dec 1945 in Belleview, Calhoun County, Illinois at age

70, and was buried in Summit Grove Cemetery.

Charles married **Mary Lee Harrison**. Mary was born in 1882 in Calhoun County, Illinois, died on 10 Jul 1948 in Belleview, Calhoun County, Illinois at age 66, and was buried in Saint Agnes Cemetery.

Children from this marriage were:

103 M   i.   **Leo Carl Foiles** was born on 3 Mar 1908 in Belleview, Calhoun County, Illinois, died on 25 Dec 1974 in Belleview, Calhoun County, Illinois at age 66, and was buried in Saint Agnes Cemetery.

104 F   ii.   **Genevieve Foiles** was born on 30 Jul 1911 in Twin Falls, Twin Falls, Idaho and died on 11 Jul 2002 in Fort Worth, Tarrant, Texas at age 90.

100. Joseph Oscar Foiles *(Daniel Webster [7], Joseph [6], John F. [5], John Jr [4], John Adam Sr (Captain) [3], Robert [2], Adam Jordan [1])* was born on 29 Dec 1877 in Calhoun County, Illinois, died in Jun 1969 in Raymond, Clark County, South Dakota at age 91, and was buried in Rose Hill Cemetery.

General Notes: Six children, three girls and three boys were born to Oscar and Jennie Foiles. The oldest, a daughter Verna, died because of ruptured appendix when she was only two and a half years old. At that time (1913) the nearest hospital was in Minneapolis, and rail was the mode of transportation to get there.

Their second daughter Mabel Christine, received her education in the Logan school and Dakota Wesleyan. She taught in rural Clark County schools before her marriage to Marvin Logan.
Alice Lucille was the third daughter in the Foiles family. She grew up and recieved her grade and high school education in Logan. She followed the teaching profession after her college days. Later she married Curtis Yates of Detroit, Michigan. She passed away there in 1972.

The three sons born to Mr. and Mrs. Oscar Foiles were Delmar
Wayne, Raymond Stenning and John Oscar. They too received their grade and high school education at Logan.

Edited from the Clark County Centennial History 1881-1981
The book is not copyrighted.

Joseph married **Jennie Susanna Stenning**. Jennie was born on 20 Oct 1883 in Clark County, South Dakota, died in 1963 in Clark County, South Dakota at age 80, and was buried in Rose Hill Cemetery.

Children from this marriage were:

105 F   i.   **Verna Foiles** was born in 1910 in Clark County, South Dakota, died in 1913 in Clark County, South Dakota at age 3, and was buried in Rose Hill Cemetery.

106 F   ii.   **Mabel Christine Foiles** was born on 14 Jun 1912 in Clark County, South Dakota, died on 29 Dec 1999 in Clark County, South Dakota at age 87, and was buried in Rose Hill Cemetery.

107 M   iii.   **Delmar Wayne Foiles** was born on 12 Aug 1915 and died on 26 Jun 2016 at age 100.

108 F   iv.   **Alice Lucille Foiles** was born on 18 Apr 1917 in Clark County, South Dakota and died in 1972 in Detroit, Michigan at age 55.

Alice married **Curtis Yates**.

109 M   v.   **Raymond Stenning Foiles** was born in 1921 in Clark County, South Dakota, died on 15 Apr 2010 in Clark County, South Dakota at age 89, and was buried in Rose Hill Cemetery.

102. Dennis Wilber Foiles *(Daniel Webster [7], Joseph [6], John F. [5], John Jr [4], John Adam Sr (Captain) [3], Robert [2], Adam Jordan [1])* was born on 8 Feb 1888 in Calhoun County, Illinois, died in Jul 1968 in Calhoun County, Illinois at age 80, and was buried in Hardin Cemetery.

Dennis married **Winnie Esther Delong**. Winnie was born on 14 May 1881 in Batchtown, Calhoun County, Illinois, died on 6 Dec 1938 in Calhoun County, Illinois at age 57, and was buried in Hardin Cemetery.

Children from this marriage were:

110 M   i.   **Ellis Merle Foiles** died on 7 Jul 1940 in Alton, Madison County, Illinois and was buried in Hardin Cemetery.

Ellis married **Anna B. Wiener**. Anna was born on 1 Oct 1908 in Calhoun County, Illinois, died on 19 Jun 2002 in Alton, Madison County, Illinois at age 93, and was buried in Hardin Cemetery.

111 M   ii. **Luther A. Foiles** was born on 17 Nov 1908 in Calhoun County, Illinois, died on 21 Sep 1951 in Pima County, Arazonia at age 42, and was buried in Hardin Cemetery.

First Generation

112. Johan Leonard Ansell was born in 1735 in Germany and died in 1805 in Virginia at age 70.

Johan married **Anna Catherina Lunn**. Anna was born in 1735 in Virginia and died in 1805 in Virginia at age 70.

The child from this marriage was:
+ 113   M   i. **Melchor Ansell** was born on 2 Feb 1780 in Germany, died on 21 Oct 1853 in Cabell County, Virginia at age 73, and was buried in Kyle Cemetery.

Second Generation (Children)

113. Melchor Ansell *(Johan Leonard [1])* was born on 2 Feb 1780 in Germany, died on 21 Oct 1853 in Cabell County, Virginia at age 73, and was buried in Kyle Cemetery.

Melchor married **Elizabeth Wentz**, daughter of **Johann Wendelinus Wentz** and **Maria Elizabeth Kirschner**. Elizabeth was born on 20 Dec 1780 in Virginia, died on 27 Apr 1858 in Kampsville, Calhoun County, Illinois at age 77, and was buried in Summit Grove Cemetery.

The child from this marriage was:
+ 114   F   i. **Hannah Ansell** was born on 1 May 1814 in Virginia, died on 23 Apr 1882 in Kampsville, Calhoun County, Illinois at age 67, and was buried in Summit Grove Cemetery.

Third Generation (Grandchildren)

114. Hannah Ansell *(Melchor [2], Johan Leonard [1])* was born on 1 May 1814 in Virginia, died on 23 Apr 1882 in Kampsville, Calhoun County, Illinois at age 67, and was buried in Summit Grove Cemetery.

General Notes: The name is also spelled Angel

Hannah married **Joseph Foiles,** son of **John F. Foiles** and **Margaret Peggy Hovermale,** on 5 Mar 1835 in Cabell County, Virginia. Joseph was born on 20 Jun 1813 in Frederick County, Virginia, died on 31 Jan 1911 in Kampsville, Calhoun County, Illinois at age 97, and was buried in Summit Grove Cemetery.

(Duplicate Line. See Person 73 on Page 35)

Hannah Ansell Foiles

First Generation

115. Johann Daniel Wiegand.

Johann married **Catharina Margaretha**.

The child from this marriage was:
+ 116 M i. **John Adam Wiegand** was born on 7 Jul 1784 in Frankfurt Am Main, Hessen, Germany and died after 1870 in Calhoun County, Illinois.

Second Generation (Children)

116. John Adam Wiegand *(Johann Daniel [1])* was born on 7 Jul 1784 in Frankfurt Am Main, Hessen, Germany and died after 1870 in Calhoun County, Illinois.

> General Notes: John Was Natrilized Jun 5 1860 In Rock Island

John married **Gertrude Hustnetter,** daughter of **Joish Hustnetter** and **M. Elisabethae Hustmutter,** on 3 Feb 1805 in Sankt Ignaz Katholisch, Mainz, Rheinhessen, Hesse-Darmstadt. Gertrude was born about 1786 in Hessen, Germany and died before 1845 in Hessen, Germany.

> Marriage Notes: Name   Joannes Adamus Weigand
> Spouse's Name   Gertrude Hustnetter
> Event Date   03 Feb 1805
> Event Place   Sankt Ignaz Katholisch, Mainz, Rheinhessen, Hesse-Darmstadt
> Citing this Record
> "Deutschland Heiraten, 1558-1929," database, FamilySearch (https://familysearch.org/ark:/61903/1:1:JHMP-XYV : 26 December 2014), Joannes Adamus Weigand and Gertrude Hustnetter, 03 Feb 1805; citing Sankt Ignaz Katholisch, Mainz, Rheinhessen, Hesse-Darmstadt; FHL microfilm 996,897.

Children from this marriage were:
117 F i. **Elisabetha Wiegand** was born on 30 Jun 1807 in Hessen, Germany.

118 M ii. **Nicolaus Wiegand** was born on 13 Aug 1809 in Sankt Ignaz, Mainz, Hessen, Germany.

119 M iii. **Petrus Wiegand** was born on 28 Feb 1814 in Sankt Ignaz, Mainz, Hessen, Germany.

+ 120 M iv. **Henry Wiegand** was born on 9 Jun 1817 in Hessen, Germany, died on 4 Mar 1882 in Calhoun County, Illinois at age 64, and was buried in Wiegand Cemetery.

121 F v. **Friedericus Wiegand** was christened on 11 Mar 1821 in Hessen, Germany.

122 M vi. **Casparus Wiegand** was christened on 23 Jun 1822 in Hessen, Germany.

123 F vii. **Elizabeth Wiegand** was christened on 11 Nov 1824 in Hessen, Germany.

John next married **Martha Emma**. Martha was born on 21 Dec 1821 and died on 23 Jul 1867 at age 45.

Third Generation (Grandchildren)

120. Henry Wiegand *(John Adam [2], Johann Daniel [1])* was born on 9 Jun 1817 in Hessen, Germany, died on 4 Mar 1882 in Calhoun County, Illinois at age 64, and was buried in Wiegand Cemetery.

> General Notes: The son of Mr. and Mrs. John Adam Wiegand, Henry was born in Hesse Capel, Germany.
> Henry's Immigration was in August 1846 on board the ship Casper he landed in Baltimore MD
>
> Henry married first and Emma Tischer in 1837 she died before 1848 then he married Martha Markhart in 1848, and they were the parents of at least 8 children, all of whom were born in the United States. Henry's widowed father lived with the Wiegands for many years. (John Adam Wiegand was born around 1784 and died in the 1870's.)
>
> The family lived in Erie County, Ohio during the early years of their marriage. They moved to Wisconsin around 1848, but only lived there a short time before arriving in Calhoun County, Illinois in 1850. Henry was a farmer.

Martha passed away in 1867 at the age of 45.

Children from first marriage: 6 sons, 4 daughters, 1 unknown infant.
Henry married Mary Barbara in the late 1860's. They did not have any children.

Children from second marriage: None.

At the time of his death, Henry was 64 years, 8 months and 23 days old. He was survived by his second wife, Mary. She married Adam J. Shiekler on 05 Apr 1883 in Calhoun County.

Father of:
William Wiegand
John Adam Wiegand
Charles Conrad Wiegand
Anna Wiegand
George Frederick Wiegand
Sarah J. Wiegand
Matilda Wiegand Smith
Albert Lafayette Wiegand
Philip K. Wiegand
Infant Wiegand
Emma L. Wiegand Jewsbury

Henry married **Martha Emma Tischer,** daughter of **Joseph Tischer** and **Agatha Lehmann,** on 13 Jun 1848 in Erie County, Ohio. Martha was born on 21 Dec 1821 in Hessen, Germany, died on 23 Jul 1867 in Calhoun County, Illinois at age 45, and was buried in Wiegand Cemetery.

Children from this marriage were:

    124   F   i.   **Anna Wiegand** was born in 1849 in Wisconsin.

    125   M   ii.   **George Frederick Wiegand** was born on 12 Dec 1850 in Calhoun County, Illinois, died on 10 Feb 1935 in Jersey County, Illinois at age 84, and was buried in Oak Grove Cemetery.

+ 126   F   iii.   **Sarah Jane Wiegand** was born on 13 Sep 1853 in Calhoun County, Illinois, died on 18 Jan 1926 in Kampsville, Calhoun County, Illinois at age 72, and was buried in Summit Grove Cemetery.

    127   F   iv.   **Matilda Wiegand** was born on 4 Dec 1856 in Calhoun County, Illinois, died on 17 Jun 1946 in Madison County, Illinois at age 89, and was buried in Hardin Cemetery.

    128   M   v.   **Albert Lafayette Wiegand** was born on 15 Jan 1859 in Batchtown, Calhoun County, Illinois, died on 5 Sep 1944 in Jersey County, Illinois at age 85, and was buried in Oak Grove Cemetery.

    129   M   vi.   **Phillip K. Wiegand** was born on 18 Apr 1861 in Batchtown, Calhoun County, Illinois, died on 25 Jan 1939 in Jersey County, Illinois at age 77, and was buried in Oak Grove Cemetery.

    130   F   vii.   **Emma L. Wiegand** was born in Aug 1865 in Calhoun County, Illinois, died on 26 Jul 1949 in Jersey County, Illinois at age 83, and was buried in Lax Cemetery.

Henry next married **Mary Barbara Niefer**. Mary was born on 27 Sep 1836 in Württemberg, Baden, Germany and died on 8 Dec 1911 in Fosterburg, Madison, Illinois at age 75.

Fourth Generation (Great-Grandchildren)

126. Sarah Jane Wiegand *(Henry [3], John Adam [2], Johann Daniel [1])* was born on 13 Sep 1853 in Calhoun County, Illinois, died on 18 Jan 1926 in Kampsville, Calhoun County, Illinois at age 72, and was buried in Summit Grove Cemetery.

Sarah Jane Wiegand
Foiles

Sarah married **Daniel Webster Foiles,** son of **Joseph Foiles** and **Hannah Ansell,** on 27 Oct 1872 in Calhoun County, Illinois. Daniel was born on 9 Jan 1843 in Cabell County, Virginia, died on 6 Sep 1933 in Kampsville, Calhoun County, Illinois at age 90, and was buried in Summit Grove Cemetery.

> Marriage Notes: Name: Daniel W Foiles
> Gender: Male
> Spouse Name: Sarah J Wiegand
> Marriage Date: 27 Oct 1872
> Marriage County: Calhoun
> Comments: This record can be found at the County Court Records, Film # 1305044 - 1305045.

(Duplicate Line. See Person 91 on Page 35)

Daniel Webster Foiles

Descendants of Joseph Tischer

First Generation

131. Joseph Tischer, son of **Antonius Tischer** and **Martha Socherin,** was born in Sep 1788 in Hessen, Germany, was christened on 2 Aug 1788 in Oberstdorf, Bayern, Germany, and died after 1860 in Ramsey, Minnisota.

> General Notes: Joseph Was Naturilized 1852
> FIRST NAME: JOSEPH
> LAST NAME: TISCHER
> LOCATION: RAMSEY
> COUNTY: RAMSEY
> STATE: Minnesota
> CODE: 36
> REEL: 11
> VOLUME: 11
> PAGE: 80

Joseph married **Agatha Lehmann**, daughter of **Andreae Lehmann** and **Annae Mariae Stahler**. Agatha was born on 10 Feb 1783 in Hessen, Germany, was christened in Gengenbach, Baden, Germany, and died after 1860 in Ramsey, Minnisota.

Children from this marriage were:

+ 132　F　　i.　**Martha Emma Tischer** was born on 21 Dec 1821 in Hessen, Germany, died on 23 Jul 1867 in Calhoun County, Illinois at age 45, and was buried in Wiegand Cemetery.

　133　F　　ii.　**Juliana Tischer**.

> Juliana married **Jakob Kaufeissen** on 27 Nov 1826 in Gengenbach, Baden, Germany.
>
> Marriage Notes: "Deutschland Heiraten, 1558-1929," database, FamilySearch (https://familysearch.org/ark:/61903/1:1:NDH5-9PK : 26 December 2014), Agatha Lehmann in entry for Jakob Kaufeissen and Juliana Tischer, 27 Nov 1826; citing Gengenbach, Baden, Germany; FHL microfilm 891,256.

Second Generation (Children)

132. Martha Emma Tischer *(Joseph [1])* was born on 21 Dec 1821 in Hessen, Germany, died on 23 Jul 1867 in Calhoun County, Illinois at age 45, and was buried in Wiegand Cemetery.

> General Notes: The family lived in Erie County, Ohio during the early years of their marriage. They moved to Wisconsin around 1848, but only lived there a short time before arriving in Calhoun County, Illinois in 1850. Henry was a farmer.
>
> At the time of her death, Martha was 45 years, 7 months and 2 days old. She was survived by her husband, Henry. He later remarried and passed away 1882.

Martha married **Henry Wiegand,** son of **John Adam Wiegand** and **Gertrude Hustnetter,** on 13 Jun 1848 in Erie County, Ohio. Henry was born on 9 Jun 1817 in Hessen, Germany, died on 4 Mar 1882 in Calhoun County, Illinois at age 64, and was buried in Wiegand Cemetery.

(Duplicate Line. See Person 120 on Page 40)

Name Index

Name Index

Name Index

Benz and Foiles
Family
Photos

Family Photos

Charles and Amanda Benz

Charles & Amanda's home on State Rd Kampsville, Illinois

OFFICE OF THE GOVERNOR
SPRINGFIELD

WILLIAM G. STRATTON
GOVERNOR

December 8, 1954

Mr. and Mrs. Charles F. Benz
Kampsville,
Illinois

Dear Mr. and Mrs. Benz:

    Mrs. Stratton and I desire to extend our congratulations and best wishes. We understand you recently observed your fifty-eighth wedding anniversary.

    Few are privileged to reach this milestone along life's pathway and I think it is remarkable that you have been blessed with each other's companionship for so many years. I hope you are both in good health and that your anniversary was a happy one.

Sincerely,

William N. Stratton

Governor

WGS:pn

Family Photos

Benz Sisters 1st Row: Mary Jane, Evadna, Wanda, 2nd Row: Wilma, Myrtle, Eula

1st Step Wanda, Myrtle 2nd Step: Mary Jane, Wilma, Evadna
3rd Row Alva, Dean

Family Photos

Mom's Sisters Eula, Wilma, Wanda and Evadna

Family Get together 1st Row: Wilma, Evadna, Wanda
2nd Row Eula, Myrtle, Mary Jane

Family Reunion Brothers & Sisters
Betsy Ann Picnic Area
L to R Dean, Evadna, Mary Jane, Myrtle (Hap)Alva, (Mom)Wanda, Eula, Wilma

Family Reunion Betsy Ann Picnic Area Wilma, Evadna

Bob & Eula (Benz) Buress

Ralph & Wilma (Benz) Haycraft

Walter & Mary Jane (Benz) Moore

This Certifies That ___Wanda Benz___ has completed in a satisfactory manner the work outlined for the Seventh Grade in the State Course of Study for the Common Schools of Illinois, and is therefore given this

Certificate of Promotion

Given at Hardin, Illinois, this ___11th___ day of ___June___ 1932

Marie Golly
TEACHER

Cuba M. Twineman
COUNTY SUPERINTENDENT OF SCHOOLS

Diploma of Graduation

Jersey Township High School
Jerseyville, Illinois

This Certifies That

Wanda L. Benz

Has satisfactorily completed the Course of Study prescribed for Graduation from this School, and is therefore awarded this Diploma.

Given this second day of June, one thousand nine hundred and thirty-seven.

B. H. Bowman
President of Board

Frank H. Markman
Principal

W. O. Wilson
Secretary of Board

CLINT W. LEE CO.

Miss Wanda Benz To Become A June Bride

Mr. and Mrs. Charles Benz of Kampsville are announcing the engagement and approaching marriage of their daughter, Miss Wanda Benz, to Raymond Roe, son of Mr. and Mrs. Claude Roe of Dow. The wedding will take place at the home of Mr. and Mrs. Ralph Haycraft, in Brighton, Saturday evening, June 15, at 7 o'clock.

Mr. Roe was separated from the U. S. Army, after 49 months of service, April 30. At the time of his separation Mr. Roe was a lieutenant.

Mr. Roe and Miss Benz are employes of Owens-Illinois Glass Co. Mr. Roe is a graduate of East Alton-Wood River High School and his fiancee was graduated from the Jersey Township Community High School.

Raymond & Wanda (Benz) Roe June 15-1946

Family Photos

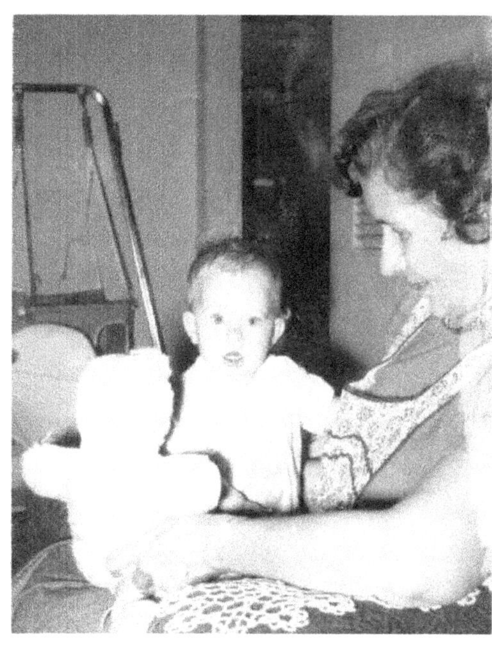

Robin & Aunt Evada

Ray, Wanda and Linda

Ray and Linda 108 Maywood

Linda at Santa Claus Land in Pikes Peake Family Trip

Linda and Robin

128 Virginia Ave Creve Coeur, Illinois 2nd Home of Ray and Wanda Roe

John, Linda, Dan 128 Virginia Ave Creve Coeur, Illinois Cousins

Family Photos

Wanda and Robin 128 Virginia Ave

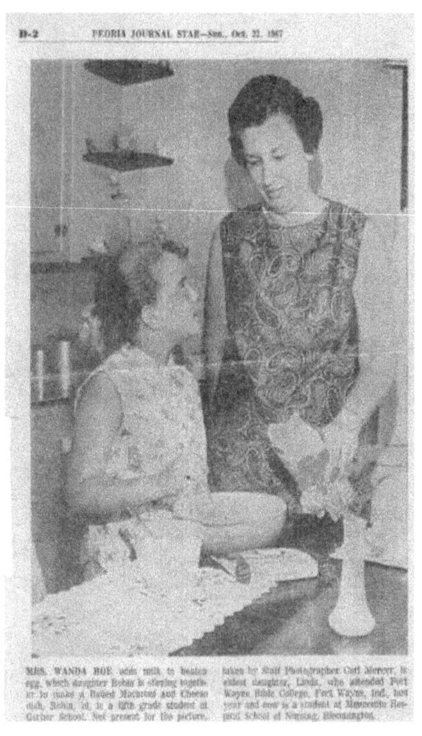

D-2   PEORIA JOURNAL STAR—Sun., Oct. 22, 1967

MRS. WANDA ROE adds milk to beaten egg, which daughter Robin is offering together to make a Baked Macaroni and Cheese dish. Robin, 10, is a fifth-grade student at Gather School. Not present for the picture, taken by Staff Photographer Carl Mercer, is eldest daughter, Linda, who attended Fort Wayne Bible College, Fort Wayne, Ind., last year and now is a student at Mennonite Hospital School of Nursing, Bloomington.

Wanda & Robin

Just Married
Wanda and Melvin Dudley
6-25-1981

Wanda in Hawaii

Rollie & Margaret Hutchison and Wanda & Mel Dudley

Wanda & Cody

Cody Benway

Lee and Robin (Roe) Benway of East Peoria announce the birth of their son, Cody Ray, born at 8:20 p.m. Aug. 18 at Methodist Medical Center in Peoria. He weighed 6 pounds, 3 ounces and was 18 inches long.

Cody was welcomed home by Toby, 17, and Shawna, 14.

Grandparents are Mrs. Wanda Dudley of Creve Coeur and Mr. and Mrs. Virgil Benway of Peoria.

Family Photos

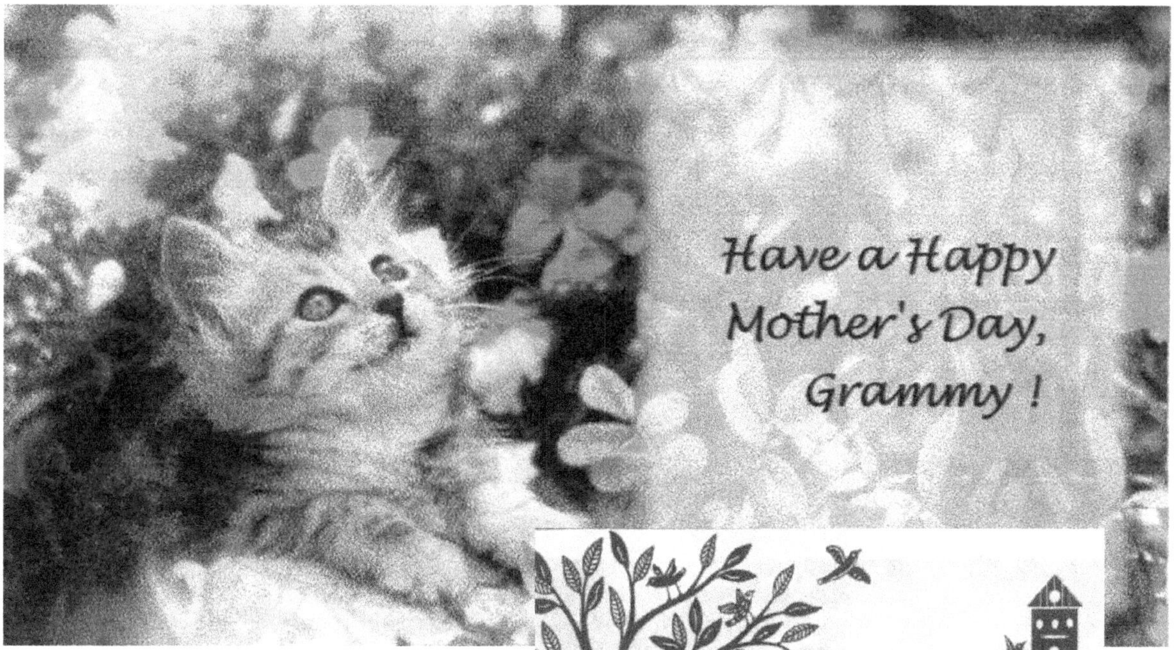

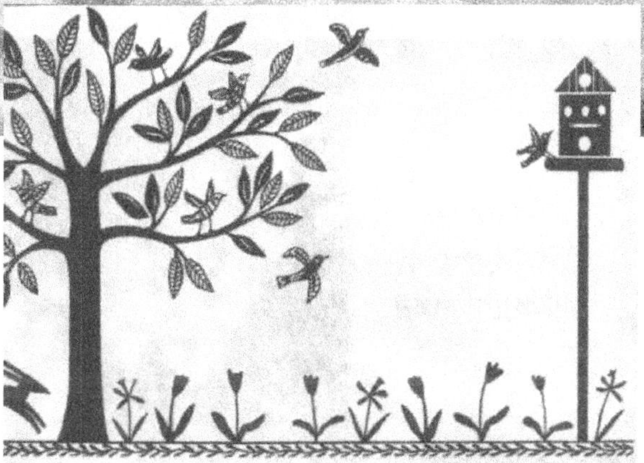

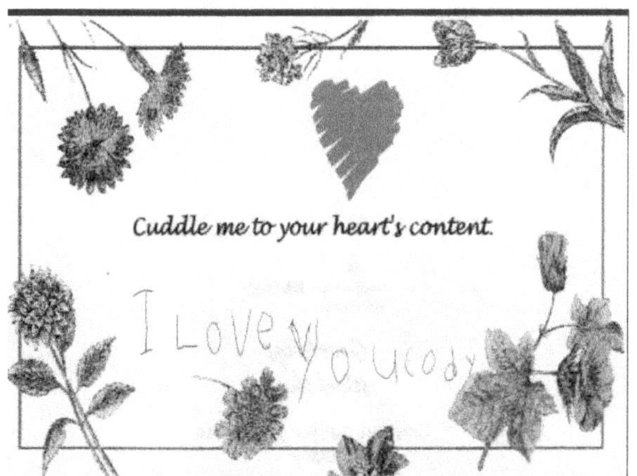

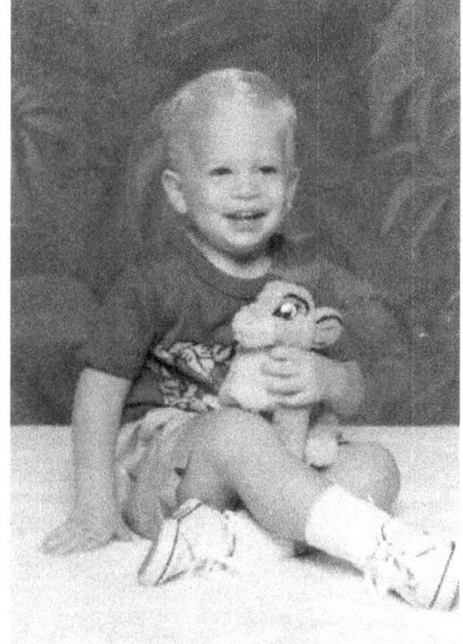

Cody and Lion King Animal

Cody at 16-17 (Mom) Wanda High School Prom

Robin's Home Thanksgiving 1st Row Robin, Mom, Linda 2nd Row Lee, Cody Harry

At Robin's Linda, Wanda, Robin Cody

Wanda at Thanksgiving

Reunion Linda, Robin, Betty, Fred, Olive Cousins 9-5-2005

Reunion at John & Kathy's L to R Harry, Linda, Robin, Cody, Lee

Family Photos

Cousin's Reunion Robin, Betty, Linda, Fred, Alice 9-11-2008

Ben, Rachel,Kathy, Nick, John, Betty, Jack, Dan, seated is John Clifford III

Family Photos

Weaubleau Mo
June 28th 1926

D. H. Foiles.

Dear Bro. & Family.

I sincerely regret that I could not attend the funeral of dear Sister Sarah. I truly sympatize in your bereavement. May God bless and keep you to the end of life. we are growing old, and our stay here on earth is coming to a close. we will meet the loved ones that have gone to Glory, and eternal rest. I pray that Gods blessings may abide with us, and watch over us: to the end. God will take of his own.

Your Brother
C. C. Wiegand

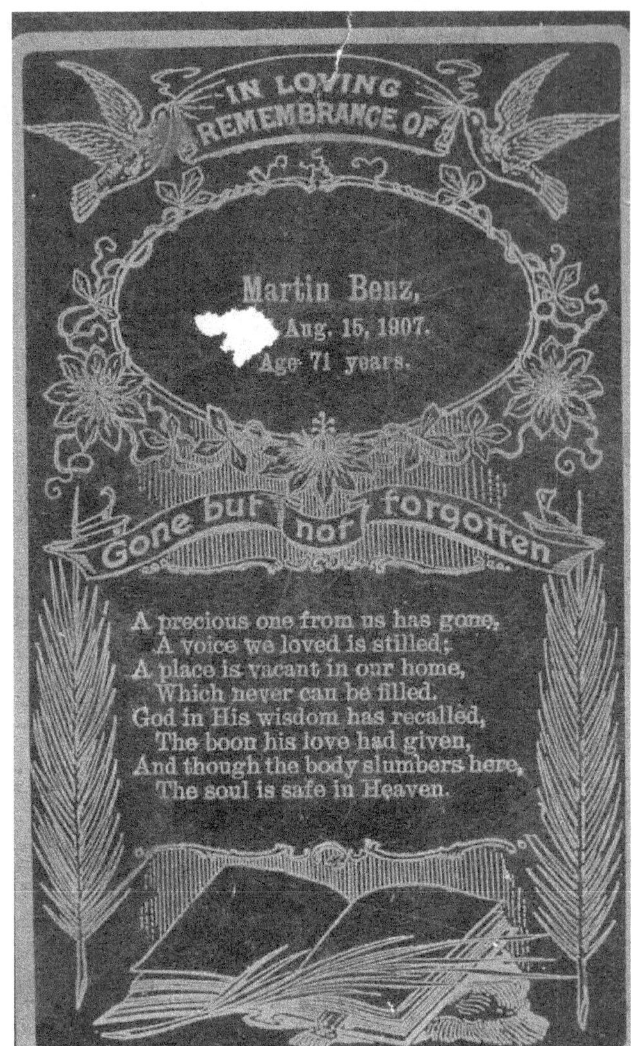

Death of Martin Benz Great Grandfather Benz

Charles F. Benz Of Near Kampsville Died Tuesday

July 26 1955

Charles F. Benz, age 84, died suddenly at his home west of Kampsville Tuesday morning at 8 o'clock. He had been in poor health for some time, but his death was unexpected. He had been up that morning and sharpened a sickle to mow some grass when he apparently became ill and went in to lie down. His wife found him a few minutes later.

Funeral services are to be held this afternoon (Thursday) at 2 p. m. (CST) in the Summit Grove Nazarene Church with Rev. W. Earl Reinbold and Rev. Ernest Rice officiating. Burial will be at Summit Grove with Hanks Funeral Service in charge.

Surviving Mr. Benz are his wife, the former Amanda Foiles, six daughters, Evadna Ball of Roxana, Eula Burris, Alton; Wilma Haycraft, Brighton, Mary Jane Moore, S. Zanesville, Ind., Wanda Roe, Creve Coeur, Ill., and Myrtle Sweetman, Hardin; and three sons, Erwin of Quincy, Alva of Alton and Dean of Brighton; he also leaves 10 grandchildren, a sister, Mrs. Emma Jackson of Columbus, Miss., and a brother, George of Carlsbad, N. M., other relatives and a host of friends.

Chas. F. Benz was born Nov. 1870 at Kampsville, the son of Martin and Mary Becker Benz. He had lived all his life in that

(Continued on page 5)

CHAS. F. BENZ OF KAMPSVILLE DIES

(Continued from page 1)

community. He married Amanda Foiles November 26, 1896 at Summit Grove.

Mr. Benz was an industrious man of great character, well liked by everyone. The News joins the many friends of the family in extending sympathy to them.

Mrs. Amanda Benz Of Kampsville Dies

Mrs. Amanda Benz of Kampsville died Monday at 9 a. m. in the Wood River Hospital, where she has been a patient for six weeks following a stroke. She was 87 years of age. Mrs. Benz had been staying with a daughter, Mrs. Evadna Ball of Roxana, when she became ill.

Surviving besides Mrs. Ball are five other daughters, Mrs. Wilma Haycraft of Brighton, Mrs. Myrtle Sweetman of Jerseyville; Mrs. Eula Burress of Alton; Mrs. Mary Jane Moore of New Boston, Ohio; and Mrs. Wanda Roe of Creve Couer, Ill., also three sons, Erwin of Quincy, Calif., Alva of Alton, and Dean of Brighton; she leaves 13 grandchildren and 10 great grandchildren; two brothers, Dennis Foiles of Hardin, and Oscar Foiles of S. Dakota, other relatives and many friends with whom the News joins in sympathy to the family. Her husband, Charles Benz, died in 1955.

Amanda Elizabeth Foiles Benz was born August 14, 1873 at Summit Grove, daughter of Daniel and Sarah Weigand Foiles, and she had lived in Calhoun most of her life. She was a member of the Church of the Nazarene at Summit Grove.

Funeral services will be held at the Summit Grove Church of the Nazarene Thursday at 2 p. m. with Rev. Floyd Comte, pastor, officiating. Burial will be in the Summit Grove Cemetery with Hanks Funeral Service in charge.

Evadna Ball

ALTON — Evadna Irene Ball, 101, died at 12:35 a.m. Wednesday, June 13, 2001, at Rosewood Care Center.

Born Sept. 3, 1899, in Kampsville, she was a daughter of the late Charles and Amanda (Foiles) Benz.

A retired schoolteacher with the Roxana School District, she was a member of the Roxana Senior Citizens and Main Street United Methodist Church.

She married Robert G. Ball July 4, 1953, in Zanesville, Ohio. He preceded her in death.

Surviving are three sisters, Myrtle Sweetman of Jerseyville, Mary Jane Moore of Lakeworth, Fla., and Wanda Dudley of Peoria; and several nieces and nephews.

She was preceded in death by two sisters, Wilma Haycraft and Eula Burress, and three brothers, Erwin, Alva and Dean Benz.

Visitation will be from 5 to 8 p.m. today at Elias-Smith Funeral Home in Alton, where services will be conducted at 10 a.m. Friday. The Revs. William Fester and Sharon Potter will officiate.

Burial will be in Summit Grove Cemetery in Kampsville.

Memorials may be given to Main Street United Methodist Church or her Sunday school class Owaisa.

Mr. And Mrs. G. Benz Celebrate Anniversary

Today is the 40th wedding anniversary of Mr. and Mrs. George R. Benz, South Highway, who exchanged nuptial vows Christmas Day, 1913 in Dexter.

Mrs. George Benz is the former Irene Shinneman and became a bride in the home of her parents, the Rev. C. C. Hill of Roswell's First Christian Church officiating.

Mr. and Mrs. Benz moved to Artesia in 1920 from Dexter, Mr. Benz being employed by the Santa Fe Railroad for 11 years. Upon their change of residence to Carlsbad in 1924 they went into the grocery and filling station business.

Six children were born to the Benz family and they now have three granddaughters and five grandsons. The children are:

Eugene Benz of Carlsbad, Mrs. Hays May of Loving, Mrs. Jack Wiseman of Carlsbad, Mrs. Lloyd Howard of Vancouver, Wash., C. A. Benz of Miami, Fla., and Mrs. Clinton Akers of St. Louis, Mo.

The three granddaughters include Linda Benz, daughter of Mr. and Mrs. Eugene Benz; Jacqueline, Jean and Peggy Wiseman. Grandsons are Bob and Jay Benz, Jimmy Wiseman, Michel Lynn May and Randy Benz, son of Mr. and Mrs. C. A. Benz.

Most of the family is home today for a family dinner at the home of Mr. and Mrs. George Benz. Friends are expected to call during the afternoon.

MR. AND MRS. GEORGE BENZ
(Framar Studio)

Obituaries

BALL

Robert Guy Ball, 78, of Roxana, Ill. died Wednesday, April 21, 1982 at St. Anthony's Hospital in Alton.

Born September 12, 1903 in Belleview, he was the son of Frank and Anna Clendenny Ball. He married Evadna Benz July 4, 1953 in South Zanesville, Ohio. He was a brickmason for Shell Oil Company retiring after 37 years of service.

Surviving besides his wife are three brothers, Ray of Hardin, Carl of Belleview and Frank of St. Louis, Mo.; three sisters, Minnie Goltz of Mozier, Flossie Nevius of Roxana, Audrey Blackstun of Alton.

Visitation was held Thursday at Smith Funeral Home in Alton.

The funeral was conducted Friday, April 10, 1982 at the funeral home with Rev. William Fester officiating. Burial was in Summit Grove Cemetery.

The Main Street United Methodist Church of Alton has been named as a memorial.

Wanda Dudley

EAST PEORIA, ILL.

Wanda L. (Roe) Dudley, 89, died at 3:43 a.m. Friday, Sept. 5, 2008, at Methodist Medical Center in Peoria, Ill.

She was born Nov 21, 1918, in Calhoun County to Charles and Amanda (Foiles) Benz.

She married Raymond Roe on June 21, 1946, in Brighton. He died July 1, 1973, in Hyden, Ky. She later married Melvin Dudley on June 15, 1981, in East Peoria. He died Sept. 10, 1991, in Peoria.

She worked in the kitchen for the Creve Coeur school district and was the cafeteria manager at Robein Grade School for nine years. She was a member of Bethany Missionary Church in East Peoria for 50 years, where she was a Sunday school teacher and a deaconess and had been involved in women's ministries.

Surviving are two daughters and their husbands, Robin and Lee Benway of East Peoria and Linda and Harry Karle of Chipley, Fla.; and her grandson, Cody Benway of East Peoria.

She was also preceded in death by her parents, five sisters and three brothers.

Visitation will be held from 5 p.m. until services at 7 p.m. Tuesday, Sept. 9, at Deiters Funeral Home in East Peoria. The Rev. Joe Weyer will officiate.

Cremation rites will be accorded. Inurnment of the cremains will be Thursday, Sept. 11, at Valhalla Memorial Park in Godfrey.

Memorials may be made to Bethany Missionary Church.

To send condolences online, visit www.deitersfuneralhome.com.

Daniel Webster Foiles

Daniel Webster and Sarah (Wiegang) Foiles

Daniel Webster Foiles and Sarah seated
LtoR   Lafayette, Joseph, Dennis, Charles, Amanda

THIS STONE COMMEMORATES:
ROBERT FOYLES & FAMILY,
SETTLEMENT OF DAVID TYGART,
FIRST ENGLISH SETTLERS WEST OF ALLEGHENIES
WESTFALL'S FORT,
BATTLE OF RICH MOUNTAIN,

Family Record

Familien=Chronik.

Erwählet euch heute, wem ihr dienen wollt . . .
Ich aber und mein Haus wollen dem HErrn dienen.

Jos. 24, 15.

Name, Geburtstag und Geburtsort des Ehemannes.

Martin Lenz geboren den 9 ten
November 1835 in Bräundlingen
Amt Donaueschingen Großherzogthum Baden

Name, Geburtstag und Geburtsort der Ehefrau.

Matilde Lenz geboren den
17 ten Februar 1850 in
Memphis, Tenn.

Memphis   Tenn   → Married

Getraut

march

am 23 ten März   1866

durch Friedensrichter Rand,

in Silver Creek, Calhoun Co. Ill.
Hardin Calhoun Co   "

Trautext:

Kinder.

Laßt die Kindlein zu mir kommen, und wehret
ihnen nicht; denn solcher ist das Reich Gottes.

Marc. 10, 14.

Louisa Wilhelmina Benz.
Born at Silver Creek, Ill.,
Jan. 17, 1867.

Theresa Benz. Born at
Silver Creek, Ill. Sept. 24, 1868.
(Deceased)

Charles Frederick Benz
Born at Silver Creek, Ill.
Nov. 24, 1870

Emma Benz. Born at
Silver Creek, Ill. Sept. 15, 1873

Kinder.

Wie sich ein Vater über Kinder erbarmet,
so erbarmet sich der HErr über die, so ihn fürchten.

Ps. 103, 13.

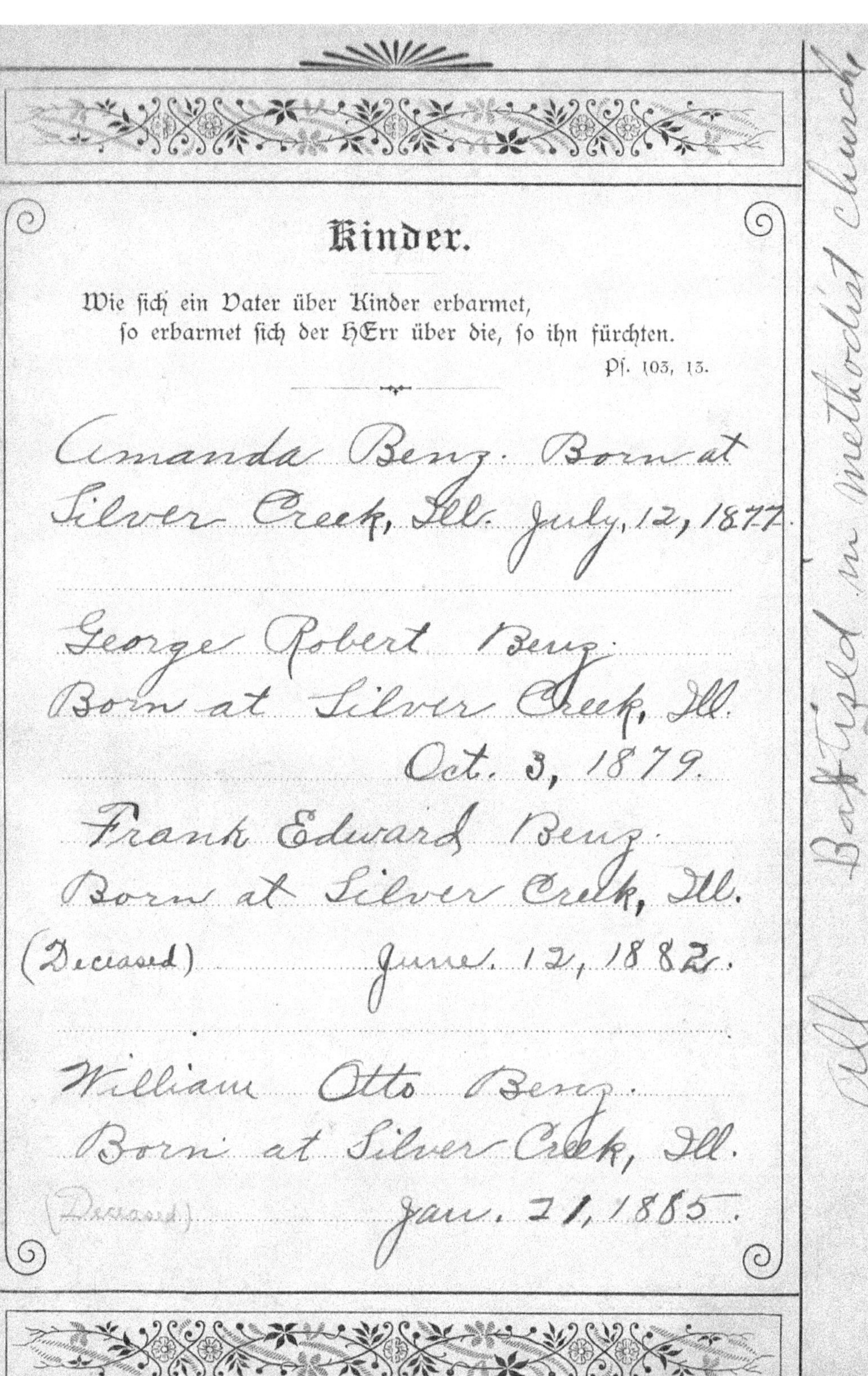

Amanda Benz. Born at
Silver Creek, Ill. July, 12, 1877.

George Robert Benz.
Born at Silver Creek, Ill.
Oct. 3, 1879

Frank Edward Benz.
Born at Silver Creek, Ill.
(Deceased)   June. 12, 1882.

William Otto Benz.
Born at Silver Creek, Ill.
(Deceased)   Jan. 21, 1885.

FAMILY RECORD.

BIRTHS.	BIRTHS.
D. W. Foiles was Born january the 9th 1842 Sarah. J. Foiles was born September the 13th 1853	

Moved August the 28 1889

Moved in the new house

FAMILY RECORD

BIRTHS.	BIRTHS.
Amanda E Foiles was born August 14th A D 1873 Charles Henry Foiles born November the 3 A D 1875 Joseph Oscar Foiles was born was born December 29 1877 Dennis Wilbur Foiles born february the 9th 1844	Philip Lafayette Foiles was born June the 28th 1886

Born 1900

FAMILY RECORD.

MARRIAGES.	MARRIAGES.
D. W. Stiles and S. A. Wiegand October 21 AD 1872	

THE

HOLY BIBLE,

CONTAINING THE

OLD AND NEW TESTAMENTS,

TRANSLATED OUT OF

THE ORIGINAL TONGUES;

AND WITH THE FORMER

TRANSLATIONS DILIGENTLY COMPARED AND REVISED

———

NEW YORK:

AMERICAN BIBLE SOCIETY,

INSTITUTED IN THE YEAR MDCCCXVI.

1867.

[Small Pica Ref.]   [Royal Octavo.]

FAMILY RECORD.

MARRIAGES.	MARRIAGES.
L. M. Stiles and S. M. Wiegand October 27 AD 1872	

Family History

Names.	Religious Persuasion	Converted or Confirmed.		Baptised.	
		When	Where	When	By Whom.
1					
2					
3					
4					
5					
6					
7					
8					
9					
10					
11					
12					
13					
14					

Names:	Cause of Death.	Where Buried.	Vault, Monument or Headstone.
1	Martin Benz — died at Kampsville, Ill. - Aug. 15, 1907		
2	Mary Matilda Benz — died at Kampsville, Ill. - Jan. 3, 1931		
3	Frank Edward Benz — died at El Reno, Okla. - Jan. 21, 1904		
4	Louisa W. Benz died at Downy, Cal. Aug 28 -		
5	1943 age 76 yrs. 7 months 19 days		
6	William Otto Benz died in St Louis		
7	Hospital		
8			
9			
10			
11			
12			
13			
14			

Family History

Children.

Names.	Born		Married.		Died.
	When	Where	When	To Whom.	
Luisa Wilhelmina Benz					
Born at Silver Creek, Ill.					
Jan. 11, 1867					
(2) Theresa Benz					
Born at Silver Creek, Ill.					
Sept. 24, 1868					
(3) Charles Frederick Benz					
Born at Silver Creek, Ill.					
Nov. 24, 1870					
(4) Emma Benz					
Born at Silver Creek, Ill.					
Sept. 15, 1873					

Names.	Nationality.	Where Educated.	Occupation or Profession.
(5) Amanda Benz			
Born at Silver Creek, Ill.			
July 12, 1877			
(6) George Robert Benz			
Born at Silver Creek			
Oct. 3, 1879			
(7) Frank Edward Benz			
Born at Silver Creek, Ill.			
June 12, 1882			
(8) William Otto Benz			
Born at Silver Creek, Ill.			
Jan. 2, 1885			

Fill out dates thus NOV. 15 1887 in small handwritings

Family Register

GRANDPARENTS

GRANDFATHER (Father's Family) GRANDMOTHER

NAME Claude Roe

DATE OF BIRTH March 24 - 1880

DATE OF DEATH July 30 - 1954

MAIDEN NAME Cora Sly

DATE OF BIRTH July 21, 1882

DATE OF DEATH March 10, 1945

GRANDFATHER (Mother's Family) GRANDMOTHER

NAME Chas. F. Benz

DATE OF BIRTH Nov. 24 - 1878

DATE OF DEATH July 26 - 1955

MAIDEN NAME Amanda Fritz

DATE OF BIRTH Aug 14 - 1878

DATE OF DEATH

PARENTS

FATHER Raymond K. Roe

BORN Oct 24, 1917 - Roodhouse, Ill. (PLACE) (DATE)

DATE OF DEATH July 1, 1973 Valhalla (BURIAL PLACE)

MOTHER Wanda L. Benz Roe

BORN Nov 21, 1918 - Kampsville, Il. (PLACE) (DATE)

DATE OF DEATH July 1, 1973 Valhalla (BURIAL PLACE)

MARRIED AT Brighton, Ill

DATE OF MARRIAGE June 15, 1946

Family Register

GRANDPARENTS

GRANDFATHER (Father's Family) GRANDMOTHER

Claude Roe

NAME

March 24 - 1880

DATE OF BIRTH

July 30 - 1954

DATE OF DEATH

Cora Ally

MAIDEN NAME

DATE OF BIRTH

DATE OF DEATH

GRANDFATHER (Mother's Family) GRANDMOTHER

Chas. F. Benz

NAME

Nov. 24 - 1870

DATE OF BIRTH

July 26 - 1955

DATE OF DEATH

MAIDEN NAME

DATE OF BIRTH

DATE OF DEATH

PARENTS

Raymond K. Roe

FATHER

Oct 21, 1917 - Roodhouse

BORN (PLACE)

July 1, 1973 Unchalk

DATE OF DEATH   BURIAL PLACE

Wanda L. Benz

MOTHER

Nov 21, 1918 - Kampsville

BORN (PLACE)

July 1, 1973

DATE OF DEATH   BURIAL PLACE

Brighton, Ill

MARRIED AT

June 15, 1946

DATE OF MARRIAGE

Fam-ily Register

CHILDREN

_____ Spencer Roe

___ 3, 19__ 8 Peoria, Ill,
PLACE

____
DATE

____
BURIAL PLACE

149 Haywood
Creve Coeur,
Ill,

___ Elizabeth Roe

__ 22, 19_5_ Peoria, Ill
PLACE

____
DATE

____
BURIAL PLACE

____
PLACE

____
DATE

____
BURIAL PLACE

____
PLACE

____
DATE

____
BURIAL PLACE

THIS IS TO CERTIFY

THAT _Raymond K. Roe_

AND _Wanda L. Berg_

WERE UNITED BY ME IN THE BONDS OF

HolyMatrimony

AT _Brighton_

ON THE _15th_ DAY OF _June_ IN THE YEAR _1946_

IN THE PRESENCE OF _Rev. C. Defoe_

SIGNED _Lee Roe_

Betty Berg Rain

THEREFORE SHALL A MAN LEAVE HIS FATHER AND
HIS MOTHER AND SHALL CLEAVE UNTO HIS
WIFE, AND THEY SHALL BE ONE FLESH.
GENESIS 2:24

Deaths

Frank Edward Berg Died at
El Reno Okla Jan. 21" 1904

Martin Berg Died at the home
of Rutger Frauenmeyer Aug. 15-1901

Matilda Berg Died at the home
of Jos. Waldheuser Jan 3" 1931

William Otto Berg Died in St.
Louis. Mo. on —

Mrs. Sarah Foiles (nee
Wiegand) Died June 18, 1926

Births

Born

Erwin Alfred Benz — Nov. 11, 1897

Evadna Irene Benz — Sept. 3, 1899

Alva Willis Benz — Feb. 13, 1901

Wilma Mildred Benz — Sept. 9, 1903

Myrtle Marie Benz — Mar. 15, 1906

Eula Maurine Benz — Sept. 2, 1908

Dean Howard Benz — Feb. 14, 1911

Mary Jane Benz — June 19, 1914

Wanda Lucille Benz — Nov. 21, 1918

Marriages

Martin Benz to Matilda
(Becker) Benz at Hardin
Calhoun Co. on 23" March
1866 By

Births
Martin Benz November
9" – 1835 at Braundlingen
and Donauschingen
capital of Baden Germany

Matilde (Becker) Benz
February 17" 1850 at
Memphis. Tenesee

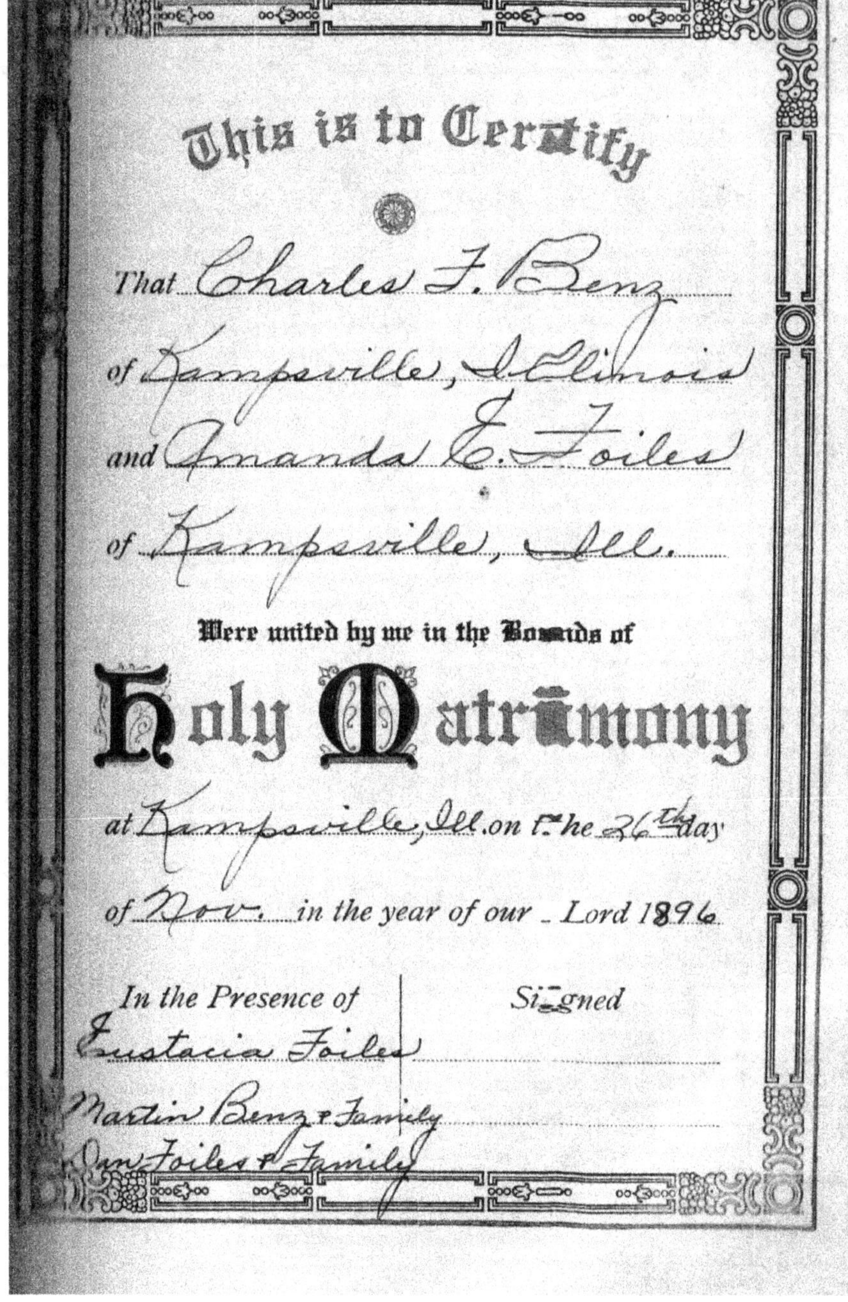

This is to Certify

That Charles F. Benz

of Kampsville, Illinois

and Amanda E. Foiles

of Kampsville, Ill.

Were united by me in the Bonds of

Holy Matrimony

at Kampsville, Ill. on the 26th day

of Nov. in the year of our Lord 1896

In the Presence of   Signed

Eustacia Foiles

Martin Benz & Family

Jim Foiles & Family

V-51-136

Family name | Given name
WIEGAND | HEINRICH

Accompanied by

Age 30 Yrs. | Sex | M. | S. ___ | Occupation | Nationality
Mos. | M | W. | D. | | MAINZ

Last permanent residence (town country, etc.) | Destination
| BALTIMOR

Port of entry | Name of vessel | Date AUGUST 5
BALTIMORE, MD. | CASPER | 1846

DEPARTMENT OF LABOR, Immigration and Naturalization Service.   Form 548-C

(34)

PETITION ADMITTING WILL TO PROBATE.

STATE OF ILLINOIS, } In the County Court. In Probate. _Febiy_ Term, A. D., 191_1_
Calhoun County.

To the Hon. _Chas E Cooke_ Judge of said Court.

The undersigned petitioner _Daniel W. Foiles_ respectfully represents to your Honor that the attached instrument of writing purporting to be the Last Will and Testament _of Joseph Foiles_ Deceased

That the said deceased departed this life at _Hamburg Precinct_

on or about the _31st_ day of _January_ A. D. 191_1_, and also that _Joseph Foiles_ at the time of h_is_ death, resided at _Hamburg Precinct_ in the County of Calhoun and State of Illinois.

Your petitioner further represents that the said _Joseph Foiles_ left, at the time of h_is_ death the following named heirs-at-law and legatees

h

no widow and

(Copy)

Last Will and Testament of
Joseph Foiles.

I Joseph Foiles of Kampsville in the State
of Illinois hereby make this my last Will
and Testament.

First) I direct that my just debts be paid
by executor hereinafter named as soon after
my death as may by them be found convenient.

Second) to my daughter Mary M. Turpin I
give and bequeath all of my property both
personal and real.

Third) My daughter Mary M. Turpin is to
pay my daughter Emily M Foiles Twelve
Hundred Dollars and keep her on said
real estate with her and her heirs as long as
she shall live.

Fourth) the said Mary M. Turpin shall pay to my
sons and daughters each Three Hundred Dollars
as follows, Jacob A. Foiles, S. W Foiles, Virginia
Sirksmeyer, America V. Nimerick.

Fifth) the said Mary M. Turpin shall pay to
my grandson Otis L. Foiles Two Hundred
Dollars.

Sixth) I hereby appoint my son S. W Foiles
as Executor of this my last Will without
giving any Bond, this date Apr. 17, 1908.

Joseph his + Foiles
mark

Alex Crader
John Sirksmeyer } witness

Last Will and Testament
of Joseph Fails

I Joseph Fails of Kampsville
in the State of Illinois hereby make
this my last Will and Testament
First) I direct that my just debts be paid
by executor hereinafter Named as soon after
my death as may by them be found convenient.
Second) to my daughter Mary M Turpin
I give and bequeath all of my Property
Both Personal and Real.
Third) My daughter Mary M Turpin
is to Pay my daughter Emily M.
Fails Twelve Hundred dollars and Keep
her on Said Real Estate with her
and her heirs as long as she shall
live.
Fourth) The Said Mary M Turpin Shall
Pay to my Sons and daughters each Three
Hundred dallers as follows. Jacob A. Fails.
L. W. Fails. Virginia Dirksmeyer.
America N. Nimerick.
Fifth) The Said Mary M. Turpin Shall
Pay to my grand Son Otis L. Fails
Two Hundred dallers.

STATE OF ILLINOIS, } ss
Calhoun County,

I _W. D. Godar_

Clerk of the Circuit Court, and ex-officio Recorder,
within and for the County and State aforesaid, do
hereby certify that the within and foregoing Instrument of Writing was filed for record on the
_6th_ day of
April A.D.
191_1_ at _10_ o'clock _A_ M.,
and duly recorded in Volume
_1_ of _Wills_
on page _73_

IN TESTIMONY WHEREOF, I
have hereunto set my hand and
affixed the seal of said Court the
day and date aforesaid.

W. D. Godar Clerk.

By ———————— Deputy.

Fee 1.00

Last Will and
Testament of
Joseph Failes

Filed Feb. 10. 1911.
John Day Jr.
Co. Clk,

Duly proved and
admitted to Record
April 3. 1911.
Chas. E. Cook
Judge

Recorded p. 146
Will Record "B"
John Day Jr.
County Clerk

NAME	State Nature of Relationship.	Post-Office Address: (If residence is unknown, then so state.)
Mary M. Turpin	Daughter	Kampsville, Ill.
Emily M. Foiles	Daughter	Kampsville, Ill.
Jacob M. Foiles	Son	Kampsville, Ill.
Virginia Sirkomeyer	Daughter	Kampsville, Ill.
America V. Nuessick	Daughter	Hamburg, Ill.
Otis L. Foiles	Grandson	Ft. Morgan, Colo.
Daniel W. Foiles	Son	Kampsville, Ill.
Amanda Perry	Daughter	Kampsville, Ill.

and that the above named persons are heirs-at-law and Legatees..

    Your petitioner further asks that the said Last Will and Testament be admitted to Probate.

          .... Daniel W. Foiles ....

Sixthly) I hereby appoint my son D. W. Foils
as Executor of this my last Will with out
giving any Bond. this date Apr 17. 1895 his
Abt Cradel) witness   Joseph + Foils
John Dicksmeyer)   mark

filing date on back

Cody Ray Benway

This is the story Cody wrote for school about his grandma. He won honorable mention in the Young Authors' competition in 5th grade.

The Life of My Grandma

In 1918 when Woodrow Wilson was president and stamps were three cents, my grandma was born. Wanda Lucille Benz was born on November 21, 1918 in Kampsville, Illinois. Kampsville is a historic river community located on the Great River Road in scenic and rural Calhoun County, a narrow peninsula between the Illinois and Mississippi River. She was born at home. Her parents were Charles and Amanda Benz. She had five sisters and three brothers. She was the youngest of nine. Their names were Erwin, Evadna, Wilma, Alva, Myrtle, Eula, Dean, Mary Jane and Wanda. Wanda was the youngest, so she got her way by crying.

Her dad was a farmer and planted 160 acres of corn and wheat plants. She lived on a farm that raised horses, cows, pigs, sheep, and chickens. She had chores like bringing in wood for the fire, milking the cows, and feeding the chickens. In her spare time, she would read with a coal oil lamp because there was no electricity at her house. Her mom made butter for 40 cents per pound for a store in town. Wanda would deliver it in cold, wet towels on the way to school.

Wanda and her friends would go to a nearby creek to swim. There were no swimsuits yet, so they wore old dresses. She could see snakes in the bushes by the creek.

Wanda had a dog named Tony. Once, her father got a new Model T Ford. Her sister mostly drove it. Wanda was going to ride in it with her mom and sister. She got in and slammed the door closed. Then she saw her dog's tail was in the door. The door broke the Tony's tail! He howled and cried and she sobbed! Another story about my grandma and her dog is how she wrapped him in a blanket and swung him on the porch swing until he threw up.

Wanda would walk to school going through a field of cows. The grades first through eighth were in the same room. When she was in the first through sixth grade her oldest sister taught her. They sat on hardwood benches. They used nickel tablets, which was paper, and penny pencils. There were no crayons or markers. The heat came from the woodburning stove. They brought lunch in buckets and ate bread and apple butter. At recess, they played tag and ball. There were no inside bathrooms, only outhouses. They had school from September to March. She walked four miles to and from school. She enjoyed reading Zane Grey cowboy stories. She loved history in high school. She played the piano a lot. She took lessons for fifty cents.

After Wanda graduated from high school, she worked at the Western Cartridge Company in Alton, Illinois in 1937. She inspected shotgun shells during World War II. There she met her first husband Raymond Keith Roe. After they were married, Ray was a brick mason and Wanda was a housewife. In 1948 they had their first child, a daughter named Linda. In 1957 they had their second daughter and they named her Robin. After Robin went to school, Wanda worked in the school cafeteria. She worked for 17 years. In 1973 on a trip to Kentucky, Ray died of a heart attack. Eight years later she married Melvin Dudley. They traveled many places during the ten years they were married. In 1991, Melvin died after surgery. Her only grandson, Cody Ray Benway was born on August 18th, 1992. Wanda stills enjoys a good life at 84 years old.

Cody loved his Grammy and we had many good times with her. It was so wonderful that we lived close and could include her in our family activities. She was a great mom, grandma and especially a woman of God. I will always treasure the time we had together!

TWITTER: @SIUSchoolofLawthird-yearstudent Cody Benway is chosen for the highly selective @TheJusticeDept Attorney General's Honors Program. [LINK] #ThisIsSIU #ThatsASaluki

FACEBOOK:@SalukiLaw third-year student Cody Benway is chosen for the highly selective and competitive @DOJ Attorney General's Honors Program. [LINK] #ThisIsSIU #ThatsASaluki

SIU law student chosen for select Justice Department program

By Pete Rosenbery

CARBONDALE, Ill. —With two summers of working in federal court-related positons behind him, SIU School of Law student Cody Benway will soon be headed to a highly selective post within the U.S. Department of Justice.

Benway recently learned he will start his post-law school legal careerparticipating in the DOJ Attorney General's Honors Program. Benway was chosen to join the Drug Enforcement Administration's Office of Administrative Law Judges as the principal law clerk to Judge Mark M. Dowd at the DEA hearing facility in Arlington, Va. A third-year law student at SIU Carbondale, Benway will take his bar exam in July after he graduates in May. He expects to start his one-year DEA judicial clerkship in early September.

The honors program has been in place since 1953 and is "recognized as the nation's premier entry-level federal attorney recruitment program," according to the DOJ website. Graduating law school students and recent law school graduates who entered judicial clerkships, graduate law programs and qualifying legal fellowships within nine months of graduating from law school are eligible.

"I was very excited just to be selected for an interview," Benway, the son of Robin and Lee Benway of Peoria,said.

Joining elite company

The competition for slots is fierce. Nearly1,600 eligible applicants sought 156 positions this year. Benway said 103 positions were for immigration-related posts, with the remaining 53 slots for other justice department divisions. Just three slots were available for DEA judicial clerkships.

"It's very selective. It's desirable. And these jobs in particular, if you have one on your resume it means that you stood out. To get selected is a big accomplishment," Ed Dawson, an assistant law professor who taught Benway in legislation and criminal procedure classes, said.

Benway's upcoming work

DEA judges sit on the only bench in the United States that presides over matters that involve administrative violations of the Controlled Substances Act and its associated regulations. As Judge Dowd's law clerk, Benway will serve as his principle legal adviser, act as the chief liaison between the court and the involved parties, and serve as Dowd's courtroom clerk. During his tenure as a law clerk, Mr. Benway will have the opportunity to travel with Judge Dowd, conducting contested administrative hearings in courthouses throughout the United States.

Known for his diligence and detailed work ethic
Benway is a "very strong student" whose attentiontodetail and diligence stands out, Dawson said. Benway is the SIU Law Journal research editor, which involves not only checking for grammar but also checking legal citations.

"It's looked at as a tedious but important task," Dawson said. "They (law journal) picked him because he's good at that sort of detail and focus and making sure citations are correct."

Benway has a "sophisticated understanding of legal issues and different solutions to legal problems," Dawson said.

Benway is also president of the law school's student chapter of the Federal Bar Association.

"He's a great student and I'm very excited that he was accepted into this program," Dawson said. "This is a good example of the opportunities students can achieve when they come here and do well."

Experiences with federal courts pays off

In summer 2016, Benway worked as law student intern with the U.S. Attorney's Office in East St. Louis. Last summer, he was a judicial extern in Peoria for Senior U.S. District Judge Joe B. McDade of the U.S. District Court for the Central District of Illinois. Benway, who is interested in being a career prosecutor and litigator, said he learned about the honors program while working in the U.S. Attorney's Office.

He credits Dawson and law professor Patricia McCubbin, who had worked with the DOJ's Environmental Defense section, with helping him prepare. Benway learned he was a finalist in October and interviewed in Washington, D.C. in early November. He received the phone call telling him of the job while driving to his parents' home in Peoria for Thanksgiving break.

"Being able to work not only behind the scenes with the judges, but with the DEA and DOJ and being able to get that first-hand experience of how it works – that will make me a more effective litigator down the road," he said.

Law school's important role in his career

Benway came to the law school after earning a bachelor's degree in criminal justice sciences from Illinois State University in 2015. He worked as a legal intern with the McLean County State's Attorney's office while in Bloomington-Normal and several prosecutors there had attended the SIU School of Law, he said.

"They had a lot of great things to say about it," he said. "That definitely drew me here."

Benway noted the "range of opportunities" that SIU School of Law students have, including the variety of available clinics that allow students to connect with attorneys in a variety of legal practices.

"It's absolutely paramount, especially at a school at this level," he said. "My relationship with Professor Dawson has helped me develop from a first-year student to where I am now. Being able to interact with all the professors in their areas of expertise, they get to know us very well and they are able to share in a more intimate relationship how we can pursue positions like this."

Paying it forward

While working for the DOJ, Benway also has plans to get the message out about the SIU School of Law. He would love to use this program to bring students to SIU and show students the opportunities that are available.